Antje Velsinger
The Bodies We Are (Not)

TanzScripte | Volume 71

Editorial

The series is edited by Gabriele Brandstetter and Gabriele Klein.

Antje Velsinger works as a choreographer, performer and researcher in the field of contemporary performing arts. She studied choreography and performance at the Institute for Applied Theater Studies at Gießen University and completed her doctorate within the artistic-scientific graduate program "Performing Citizenship" at HafenCity University Hamburg. As the artistic director of "Antje Velsinger / new trouble", she creates multimedia stage pieces, sound-video-installations, and various research labs. Besides her artistic work, her practice includes writing, teaching, and lecturing at different European universities and art schools.

Antje Velsinger
The Bodies We Are (Not)
A Choreographic Research on Practicing Self-Distancing

[transcript]

This research work has been submitted and accepted as a dissertation under the title "The bodies we are (not). A choreographic research on practicing self-distancing" at the HafenCity University Hamburg in the graduate school Performing Citizenship.

Bibliographic information published by the Deutsche Nationalbibliothek
The Deutsche Nationalbibliothek lists this publication in the Deutsche Nationalbibliografie; detailed bibliographic data are available in the Internet at https://dnb.dnb.de/

© 2024 transcript Verlag, Bielefeld

All rights reserved. No part of this book may be reprinted or reproduced or utilized in any form or by any electronic, mechanical, or other means, now known or hereafter invented, including photocopying and recording, or in any information storage or retrieval system, without permission in writing from the publisher.

Cover layout: Maria Arndt, Bielefeld
Cover illustration: "Let's face it", Sophie Aigner / Antje Velsinger
Proofread: Gregory Bogle

https://doi.org/10.14361/9783839470909
Print-ISBN: 978-3-8376-7090-5
PDF-ISBN: 978-3-8394-7090-9
ISSN of series: 2747-3120
eISSN of series: 2747-3139

Contents

Acknowledgement 7

1. Introduction
Optimization as well as self-expression –
about the role of the body in the Western neoliberal society 9

2. State of the Art... 29
2.1 Sociological perspectives on the body as a medium
and place for self-formation 34
2.2 Self-formation in contemporary dance practice
and choreography 42

3. On Methods
The gap between what we are & what we are not 55

4. The first artistic research project "The bodies we are"...................... 63
4.1 Preparing the research. A collection of bodies we are not 64
4.2 Theoretical perspective: How the body image can be influenced by action
and perception 66
4.3 Artistic experiments: Appropriating unfamiliar actions and perceptions 69
4.4 Theoretical perspective: How the body image can be influenced by labeling
and naming 77
4.5 Artistic experiments: Appropriating unfamiliar body descriptions 82
4.6 Theoretical perspective: The creative gap between sensory perception
and processes of naming 95
4.7 Artistic experiments: Appropriating an unfamiliar method.
The body image as a role in Method Acting 98

    4.8 Conclusion first research project: The body as a sensitive container 111
    4.9 Sharing the first artistic research project with an audience 114

**5. A historical perspective on the body
and the ability to play with self-distancing** 125
    5.1 The body as something natural and impersonal
in the Ancien Régime of the 18th century 126
    5.2 The body as an expression of the inner self in the 19th century 129
    5.3 The non-social but intimate body in the 20th and early 21st century 132

6. The second artistic research project "Let's face it!" 137
    6.1 Preparing the artistic research... 138
    6.2 Artistic experiments: On a face without a body 143
    6.3 Theoretical perspective: Play as a process taking place "in between"........... 148
    6.4 Artistic experiments: On a body with plenty of faces & bodies without faces 150
        6.4.1 The practice of vanishing 152
        6.4.2 The practice of perceptual transformation 160
        6.4.3 The practice of playfully falling into and out of faces 165
    6.5 Conclusion - Second research project 172
    6.6 Sharing the second research project with an audience........................173
    6.7 Reflections on the utopian potential of playing with self-distancing 184

7. Conclusion..187

References 199
Image Credits 206

Acknowledgement

First and foremost, I would like to thank my research supervisors Prof. Dr. Mirjam Schaub, Dr. Kerstin Evert and Prof. Nik Haffner for their profound support and generosity. Without their constructive and inspiring feedback and encouragement, this work would not be what it is now. I also want to thank Sophie Aigner, Lena Lessing, Juli Reinartz, Johanna Roggan and Vania Rovisco for contributing their expertise as co-researchers in the artistic research projects. Their openness, curiosity and dedication were a great support.

I also thank the artistic institutions that supported my research: K3 – Center for Choreography | Tanzplan Hamburg (Dr. Kerstin Evert and team) as well as Tanzfaktur Cologne (Slava Geppner and team) supported the artistic research projects with rehearsal space, technical support and constructive feedback. I also thank the team of PACT Zollverein, especially Simone Graf and Stefan Hilterhaus, for supporting my artistic research with two residencies which not only offered financial support, but also implied inspiring discussions and feedback on the practical experiments. Many thanks go to my colleagues and the professors at the postgraduate program "Performing Citizenship" which provided the supportive frame in which this research could be realized. For their constructive feedback in the process of writing this thesis, I thank Heike Bröckerhoff, Irene Schaefer and Benjamin Velsinger. For proof reading and English language advice, I would like to thank Irene Schaefer, Benjamin Velsinger and Gregory Bogle.

Over the course of working on this thesis, I shared and discussed my thoughts, ideas, doubts and questions in numerous talks with colleagues and friends who helped me to develop these thoughts. I thank Ayla Pierrot Arendt, Jenny Beyer, Sebastian Blasius, Verena Brakonier, Heike Bröckerhoff, Eva Burghardt, Caroline Byström, Thari Jungen, Moritz Frischkorn, Paula Hildebrandt, Katarina Kleinschmidt, Lea Moro, Katharina Pelosi, Liz Rech, Martin Sonderkamp, Benjamin Velsinger, Ursina Tossi and the late Anaïs

Rödel. Finally, I want to thank my family and friends for their love, support and patience. Without them, this work would not exist.

1. Introduction
Optimization as well as self-expression – about the role of the body in the Western neoliberal society

Ever since humans in the Western world started to actually think about the human body, it has always been a paradoxical issue. Because of its very nature, the body automatically exists as subject as well as object[1]. As a subject, the body equals something that an individual is, it is the place from where one sees, feels, smells and hears the world and, therefore, it is the home of the individual's consciousness and mind. As an object, however, it equals something the individual has and as such, it consists of matter, i.e., flesh, bones, organs, hormones, etc. Because of the fact that human individuals, in comparison to other species, can consciously perceive their own body as an object, they are able to develop the capacity of reflecting on their body.[2] Considering the body as twofold, i.e. as a subjective and objective reality, the "self" can be defined as the unity of the body subject and the body object.[3] This particular understanding of the body as something that, as a subject, is the home of the individual's experiences and, as an object, is something the individual can actively form and also reflect on, is the base from which my research starts. Because of this double nature of the human body, in the context of this work, I consider the body as a medium and place for individual self-expression.[4]

---

1 This particular understanding of the body is central to phenomenology. Cf. for example Plessner, Helmuth (2003) Conditio Humana.
2 Cf. Gugutzer, Robert (2002) Leib, Körper, Identität, p. 65.
3 Cf. Gugutzer (2002), p. 67.
4 The body as object can be consciously formed and manipulated and can therefore be used as a MEDIUM for self-expression. Since this active use of the body as object can simultaneously be perceived from the internal perspective of the body as subject, the

According to the philosopher Michela Marzano, the current Western discourse on the body seems to be trapped.[5] Despite all present attempts at defining the human being as a unity of body and mind, according to Marzano, the former dualism between ephemeral body and eternal mind has never been completely eradicated. However, at the beginning of the 21st century, this dualism seems to be meeting with a new interpretation; it is now considered to be a dualism between body and willpower.[6] Marzano states that in the Western neoliberal society, especially in the social middle class, the attitude towards the body is highly contradictory: On the one hand, the body is considered as an object that can be formed and manipulated, on the other it is considered as the reality that subjects individuals to death. On the one hand, there is a "Körpertotalität"[7] (body totality), which equates the body with identity, while on the other hand, the body is considered a reality that many believe they can keep at bay – be it through new technological possibilities or through the omnipotence of non-bodily willpower.

Based on the sociological assumption that the way individuals think about and use their bodies is related to the particular norms and values of their respective social environment[8], the sociologist Paula Irene Villa broaches the issue of body and willpower in relation to the Western neoliberal middle class

---

body is also the PLACE where this self-expression shows itself. Since both, how the body is used and how the body perceives its own self is open to change, in the context of this work, the body is not considered as a stable unchangeable entity, but as a reality that is open to change and transformation.

5 Cf. Marzano, Michela (2013) Philosophie des Körpers, p. 10.
6 Cf. Marzano (2013), p. 27.
7 Cf. Marzano (2013), p. 10.
8 As the sociologist Robert Gugutzer states, the body is viewed as a societal phenomenon in two regards: one, as a product of society, and two, as a producer of society. The human body is a product of society in the sense that our handling, our knowledge, our feeling and our pictures of the body are defined by societal structures, values, norms, technologies, and systems of ideas. On the other hand, the human body is a producer of society because our living together, our social organization, is essentially affected by the physicalness of socially acting individuals. Social reality results from social actions, and social action always involves bodily action. Therefore, bodily (inter-)actions play a crucial part in the construction of social reality. Cf. Gugutzer, Robert (2015) Soziologie des Körpers, p. 8f.

society with its core norms and values of individual autonomy, self-responsibility and self-optimization.[9]

According to Villa, in the particular context of the Western neoliberal society, the individual body is used as "raw material" for self-design[10], while this self-design meets with the neoliberal request of self-enhancement and self-optimization.

The particular practices that are used to work on the body are manifold and can be found in different fields, such as the fitness industry, health-app-suppliers, plastic surgery, the pharmaceutical industry, the cosmetics industry, the (super-)food industry, etc.[11] Those fields offer plenty of different services, such as: Clothing, Hairstyling and Make Up. Pills for optimal concentration and fearless openness; lasered eyes; tightened tendons and optimized oxygen reception in the blood for enhanced athletic performance; wrinkle-free skin and ideal body forms through plastic surgery; risk-free births and "tailormade", defect-free children through genetic engineering. Sociologist Anke Abraham states that, in today's neoliberal, capitalist society, every aspect of human life not only can, but – more worryingly – also should or even must be enhanced, rebuilt, and perfected through the use of biotechnology.[12]

As diverse as the methods and practices of forming and manipulating the body as a designable object are, their promises are similar – namely to form, manipulate, and optimize the individual body according to the particular individual's own willpower. As Villa suggests, those different practices of forming and manipulating the body predominantly happen in the mode of hard work on the own self.[13]

---

9   Cf. Villa, Paula-Irene (2008a) Wider die Rede vom Äußerlichen. In: Villa, Paula-Irene (ed.) Schön normal. Manipulationen am Körper als Technologien des Selbst.
10 Cf. Villa, Paula- Irene (2013) Prekäre Körper in prekären Zeiten – Ambivalenzen gegenwärtiger somatischer Technologien des Selbst, p. 66 In: Mayer, Ralf; Thompson, Christiane; Wimmer, Michael (eds). Inszenierung und Optimierung des Selbst. Zur Analyse gegenwärtiger Selbsttechnologien.
11 Cf. Villa (2008a), p. 11.
12 Cf. Abraham, Anke (2010) Körpertechnologien, das Soziale und der Mensch. In: Abraham, Anke; Müller, Beatrice (eds.) Körperhandeln und Körpererleben, p. 113.
13 Cf. Villa, Paula-Irene (2008b) Habe den Mut, Dich deines Körpers zu bedienen, p. 260 In: Villa, Paula-Irene (ed.) Schön normal. Manipulationen am Körper als Technologien des Selbst.

Therefore, one can argue that, in Western neoliberal society, especially in the social middle class[14], forming and manipulating the body according to one's own will is not a neutral territory potentially open to any possible direction of the individual's own idea. In fact, as sociologist Ulrich Bröckling points out, the neoliberal norms of self-determination, self-responsibility, and self-optimization create a social environment in which those who do not continuously work on the enhancement of the own body, i.e., on the own self, do not deserve any approval.[15]

According to the sociologist Robert Gugutzer, the particular role of the body in the individual search, construction, and expression of the own identity[16] actually emerged as a reaction to the social process of individualization taking place in the course of the last third of the 20th century.[17] In this process of individualization, a cultural change of values took place, including a shift from values of duty and obedience to values of autonomy and self-realization, from disciplinary to hedonistic, from material values (income, career) to immaterial values (lust for performance, fun).[18] This is when traditional social orientation had become unreliable so that orientation needed a different source. As Gugutzer states, it is for this reason that the body, i.e., something that is always present and that one can always take hold of, turned into a central place for identification. There, one's own agency could be performed, since working on one's own body could produce direct and immediately perceptible effects.

---

14   As the sociologist Alkemeyer points out; In der postindustriellen Leistungsgesellschaft ist der Körper vor allem in den aufstiegsorientierten Sozialmilieus der Mittelklassen zu einem Medium avanciert, an dessen Modellierung die Hoffnung geknüpft ist, eine ganzheitliche, das Innere wie Äußere einer Person betreffende Selbstformierung zu erreichen. Cf. Alkemeyer, Thomas; Budde, Gunilla; Freist, Dagmar (eds.) (2013) Einleitung, p. 13. In: (dies.): Selbstbildungen. Soziale und kulturelle Praktiken der Subjektivierung.

15   Cf. Bröckling, Ulrich (2007) Das unternehmerische Selbst

16   Cf. Gugutzer (2015), p. 42f. In the context of this work, I consider identity with Robert Gugutzer as something that is intrinsically tied to the body. Gugutzer defines the human 'self' as a unity of the body's perceptive and sensitive dimension, and of the body's reflecting dimension. The forming of an identity and of the self is the result of an interplay between physical experience and language-based processes of active reflection, with Gugutzer defining identity as the preliminary result of physical experiences, that are potentially subject to change. Cf. Gugutzer (2002), p. 15ff, p. 300.

17   Cf. Gugutzer (2015), p. 42.

18   Cf. Gugutzer (2015), p. 42.

1. Introduction

In the particular social context of Western neoliberal society, the combination of considering the body as a designable object and simultaneously considering it to be a place where the own identity is preferably constructed carries a number of problems in its wake. Obviously, the interest in both forming and manipulating the body and considering the body the home of the individual experience are not exclusively linked to the present Western neoliberal society. As stated above, both considerations are a result of the twofold nature of the human body, and accordingly, they can be found in a broad variety of cultural and historical contexts.

However, as Abraham states, in the present context of Western neoliberal society, the imperative of self-enhancement radically narrows down how bodies are potentially formed.[19] In this context, the ways of handling the individual body are closely tied to working and optimizing the body from the very beginning[20], aiming at erasing all aspects of the body that do not fit the neoliberal imperative of self-enhancement, such as age, disease, laziness, or atony.[21] And although critical discourses also exist, such as the body-positivity movement[22] which fights for the abolition of unrealistic and discriminating beauty ideals, the neoliberal request for self-enhancement and self-optimization is still a reality that individuals are confronted with on a daily basis. In this context, social media platforms, such as Instagram or TikTok, play a key role by directly or indirectly confronting the platforms' app users with particular beauty ideals.

Therefore, one can conclude that working and optimizing the body within the neoliberal context must be understood as a highly normative work. As Abraham puts it, deviations from the socially preferred optimized body create a feeling of defect, thus creating a need for correcting and optimizing the body.[23] Hence, one can conclude that within the neoliberal social environment, where enhancement and optimization pervades all spheres of public and private domains, the unreflected belief in the body as a designable object, while simultaneously considering it as "identity-project"[24], leads to a situation

---

19   Cf. Abraham, Anke; Müller, Beatrix (2010) Körperhandeln und Körpererleben. Einführung in ein brisantes Feld. In: dies. (eds.) Körperhandeln und Körpererleben, p. 10 f.
20   Cf. Villa (2008b), p. 266.
21   Cf. Alkemeyer, Thomas; Budde, Gunilla; Freist, Dagmar (eds.) (2013), p. 13.
22   Cf. for example Cwynar-Horta, Jessica: The Commodification of the Body Positive Movement on Instagram. In: Stream: Inspiring Critical Thought. 8, Nr.2, 2016, p. 36–56.
23   Cf. Abraham, Anke; Müller, Beatrix (2010), p. 28.
24   Cf. Gugutzer (2015), p. 45.

where it becomes more and more difficult for the individual to rest, vanish, or recover from the social demand of optimization. This missing break in the social demands becomes especially problematic when the social impositions of optimization and control cannot be fulfilled, i.e., when bodies become old, sick, or when bodies simply look different or behave differently than the norm.

What is also problematic in this context is the fact that the social imperative of enhancing and optimizing the body, in order to express the own identity can most easily be adopted by and adapted to only by people with a more substantial financial background.[25] For this reason, especially the neoliberal rhetoric of the free choice of self-realization is problematic, since it veils the prerequisites of privilege, time, and money that many people cannot fulfill. Thus, they are barred from applying those practices and techniques – which obviously, in turn, provokes social segregation.

Based on those critical observations, there are plenty of voices within the recent sociological and philosophical discourse on the body that search for an alternative approach to the body within the actual context of neoliberal society. The philosopher Marzano, for example, asks how one could create a philosophy of the body which identifies the meaning and merit of physicality.[26] The sociologist Anke Abraham critically raises the question of what individuals actually gain by constantly working on their own self-enhancement.[27] In order to find a different, more appreciating approach to the body, Abraham proposes to create manifold and satisfying opportunities for concrete, practical experiences in which individuals can enjoy the potency of their body.[28] Similar to Abraham, the activist and writer Silvia Federici also claims a re-appropriation of the body by acknowledging the power and wisdom of the physical body.[29] In her thinking, Federici proposes an entirely different perspective on the human body by considering it no longer as a separated individual, but as something that is connected to all other existing organisms on the planet.

This alternative approach to the body, that Marzano, Abraham, Federici and many others are interested in, could also be described as an interest in

---

25   Cf. Marzano (2013), p. 26.
26   Cf. Marzano (2013), p. 7.
27   Cf. Abraham (2010), p. 128.
28   Cf. Abraham (2010), p. 131.
29   Cf. Federici (2020) Jenseits unserer Haut. Körper als umkämpfter Ort im Kapitalismus. p. 12f.

the question of how one could emancipate the body from the neoliberal imperative of self-enhancement. Besides the idea to explore alternative ways of being in the body, the question how this alternative approach could look like on a practical level, is not finally answered yet.

As a choreographer[30], I observe the social discourses on the body that I have presented above with interest as well as a certain disagreement and discomfort. In my artistic work as a choreographer, I, too, am very much interested in processes of forming and creating bodies, but less with the aim of optimization and enhancement, but rather with an interest in playing, examining, or discovering a body's scope of potential. But there is another difference between my choreographic approach to form and create bodies and the practices of body optimization that I described above. Unlike the practices offered by health-app-suppliers, plastic surgery, or the pharmaceutical industry, my choreographic interest does not imply a physical intervention into the physical structure like, for example, an operation. Rather, my choreographic approach involves a process of creating and forming the internal body image of the performers.

When I speak about the internal body image in the context of this work, I refer to a concept by the phenomenologist Shaun Gallagher, which is based on the phenomenological understanding that the body consists of a subjective and an objective reality. According to Gallagher, the internal body image includes three different aspects[31]: Firstly, it includes how the body is perceived in the immediate consciousness. This aspect is connected to the individual perception of the body as a subject. Secondly, it includes the conceptual construction of the body. This aspect is connected to language and the particular way in which an individual, but also the social discourse the individual is situated in speaks about and reflects on the body.

And thirdly, it includes the emotional attitude and feelings towards the body. This third aspect is also connected to the individual perception of the body as subject.

---

[30] As any art form, choreography implies diverse approaches and practices. On a basic level, choreography could be understood as an artistic practice of framing how human and non-human bodies move in time and space. For a detailed overview of diverse contemporary understandings of choreography also see: https://www.corpusweb.net/was-ist-choreographie.html (date accessed 5 January 2022)

[31] Cf. Gallagher, Shaun (1986) Body image and body schema. A conceptual clarification. p. 545f. In: Journal of Mind and Behaviour, Vol.7, No. 4.

Accordingly, when I – as a choreographer – refer to my interest in actively forming and creating bodies within an artistic process, I do not refer to interventions in the body's matter, but I refer to an interest in exploring different strategies of manipulating the internal body images of the dancers and performers with whom I work. This process involves three different aspects: Firstly, I experiment with different internal focuses on, for example, particular body parts, physical relations between body parts or areas, or on particular sensual phenomena, in order to manipulate how the dancer or performer subjectively perceives his or her own body. Secondly, I use language and naming of particular body parts, a physical state, etc., as a tool to create alternative conceptual constructions of the body. Thirdly, I explore different ways of using movement and language to influence the emotional feelings in the individual perception of the performer.

In my choreographic practice, those three aspects are intertwined with and also influencing each other. As all three aspects are open to change, the internal body image is not stable, but something that is open to change and transformation. In the choreographic process, this process of forming and creating an internal body image produces physical movement. Accordingly, within the artistic process, the dancers or performers translate their perceptions and sensations as well as the labels into movement and performative actions. Through this performative translation, internal

body images show themselves in time and space and thus can be perceived by an outside spectator.

To contextualize my choreographic interest in forming and recreating body images as a tool to initiate and develop choreographic movement, one also needs to consider the particular way I was educated within the contemporary dance[32] context. In the contemporary dance context, there is not only one single way of understanding, using, and training the body. Accordingly, there exists a broad variety of different methods and approaches to working with the body, ranging from somatic practices such as Body-Mind-Centering[33],

---

32   Contemporary dance as an art form can be characterized as a diffusion of heterogeneous dance styles and choreographic practices. Thus, in contrast to classical, modern or post-modern dance, contemporary dance cannot clearly be categorized. As Sybille Dahms states: Contemporary dance rather expresses an attitude towards movement that conceives the constant change of form and thoughts as its essence. Cf. Dahms (2001) Tanz (Kassel: Bärenreiter), p. 181.

33   Cf. for example Hartley, Linda (1995) Wisdom of the body moving: an introduction to body-mind centering

Feldenkrais[34], or Klein-Technique[35], to different Release-Techniques[36], Yoga, to Contemporary-Ballet-Techniques[37]. Each of those methods has a different effect on the perception as well as on the physicality of the body. While the somatic practices focus on internal bodily sensations and perceptions, which then create corresponding forms and movement qualities, other movement practices such as Yoga, and Contemporary-Ballet-Techniques quite by contrast focus on working with pre-set forms and movement sequences and then expect them to produce particular physical sensations and experiences. Comparing the different approaches one can say that the different movement practices entail different body images as well as different approaches of setting the body into movement, including also partly different vocabulary to speak about the body as well as focusing on creating different internal bodily sensations and perceptions.

Depending on which movement practice is used, the particular perception of the body itself as well as the body's movement can be radically different. In the educational context, a dance student could, for example, start the day with a Klein-Technique class. In this class, the teacher would guide the class through different exercises, focusing on the scope of bones, especially on the connection between sitting bones and heels. Thus, in this class, the dance student would be encouraged to intensely focus on the skeleton of the body, i.e. on his or her individual perception on the scope of bones. This class could be followed by a BMC class, where the teacher might focus on the scope of skin, offering different exercises to the dance students in which they can explore the organ of skin whilst moving. In the first class, the perspective on the body would be linked to a structural, bony, architectural perception of the body, whereas in the second class, the body would be considered as a sensuous surface, or as a permeable border between inside and outside. Since both classes would focus on entirely different internal body sensations and perceptions, they would also most likely lead to different movements and movement qualities, that could also be perceived as clearly different from the outside perspective of a spectator.

---

34   Cf. for example Beringer, Elizabeth (ed) & Feldenkrais, Moshe (2010) Embodied wisdom: the collected papers of Moshe Feldenkrais
35   Cf. www.kleintechnique.com (date accessed 5 January 2022)
36   Cf. for example Diehl, Ingo & Lampert, Friederike (ed) (2011) Dance techniques 2010 – Tanzplan Deutschland
37   Cf. for example Forsythe, William (2012) Improvisation Technologies. A tool for the analytical dance eye

Since contemporary dancers train themselves in such a variety of different practices, the dance scientist Susan Foster states that the "selves" of contemporary dancers are aesthetically unspecific and highly flexible.[38] Considering the self as an unity of body subject (the area of subjective sensuous perception) and body object (the area of intentional objective use, reflection, processes of naming), one can conclude that, through the particular training within the contemporary dance field, dancers learn to consciously change between different ways of perceiving and reflecting on the individual body. In contemporary dance, thinking body and self as something flexible involves a process of constantly searching for alternative potentials of the individual body. If one relates this practice to the norms and values of the Western neoliberal society, one could state that this particular training also prepares dancers to adapt to any demands coming from capitalist society.

The concept of a body image that is open to change, and therefore can be actively created is the precondition to each of my own choreographic projects as well. Here, the process of consciously creating and recreating body images goes along with an interest in researching on particular topics or questions. In this context, I consider the body as the place, where this research is conducted. As a contemporary choreographer, I do not aim at developing a fixed movement vocabulary. This is why, instead, my focus is on developing the movement material from the particular topic chosen. In order to do this, I have to transfer my topic and my questions onto the body so that the body and its movements become the active place where questions and issues can be investigated and negotiated. In this choreographic approach, conceptual questions are transformed into physical questions[39].

---

38 Cf. Foster, Susan (2006) Dancing Bodies. In: Desmond, Jane (ed.): Meaning in Motion. New Cultural Studies of Dance, p. 241.

39 On the practical level, I consider choreography as a tool to consciously initiate movement in human and/or non-human bodies. In this process of initiating movement, I rarely confront bodies with fixed movement- or step sequences, or pre-set space- and/or time patterns. I rather initiate and develop movement by creating relationships between the dancer's bodies and something else, such as an object, an idea, a concept, an imagination, a quality, an internal anatomical structure or connection, an intention, a specific spatial or temporal structure, an emotional state, a timing, etc. The movement material generated in the exploration of one or also various relationships can be considered the result of this encounter. Although the movements that are created in this process are not pre-determined, they are not arbitrary, but rather the result of a specific frame I create as a choreographer. This frame, which implies bringing the dancer's bodies in relationship with something specific, is always re-

In this context, I consider choreography as a critical tool to actively take part in creating alternative discourse on the body.[40] Following Andrew Hewitt's proposal of thinking choreography as both a social and aesthetic practice[41], choreography does not exist independently from social norms and structures of its particular social environment. Accordingly, choreography is not just another thing we do to bodies, but also a reflection on, and enactment of, how bodies do things.[42] In this particular understanding, as Hewitt states, choreography can be considered as a grey zone where discourse meets practice, with this grey zone offering a possibility for critique, since artists can use choreography to develop and rehearse alternative ways for using and reflecting on bodies.

Comparing the choreographic approach to the body with the neoliberal interest in using the body as a medium[43] and place for self-enhancement and optimization, what is alike is the underlying interest in the body as something that is open to change and transformation. In the neoliberal social context, how the body is formed and created is predominantly goal oriented and follows the aim of enhancement, whereas in the choreographic context, forming and creating body images does not follow a general pre-set goal. Here, the process of creating body images is connected to the particular artistic interest of an individual artist or a group of artists and to the specific topic or question they are working on. Accordingly, one can state that the choreographic field – even though situated within the same neoliberal social context itself – offers the artists a space of action that is much wider than in everyday social contexts. In this space of action, artists can actively and consciously make deci-

---

lated to the specific interest or topic I work on. Within the choreographic process, it is very important for me to be transparent about the reasons or decisions for a specific frame. It is important for me that the dancers take the frame as something they can use in a self-determined way to initiate movement in and with their bodies, by consciously playing with their own perception, their own potentials of movement, and their way of thinking during the exploration process.

40   Cf. Hewitt, Andrew (2005) Social Choreography. Ideology as Performance in Dance and Everyday Movement, p. 15.
41   Cf. Hewitt (2005), p. 19.
42   Cf. Hewitt (2005), p. 15.
43   When I speak about the body as a medium in the context of this work, I do not refer to media theory, but to a phenomenological concept of the body which considers the body as both object and subject. Based on this understanding, the body is considered as a medium and place for individual self-expression. Also cf. p. 9 of this paper.

sions on what kind of body images are actually created and performed, while in this process, it becomes possible to play with social norms.

Based on this observation, the starting question of my research was: How could the choreographic field be used when emancipating the body from the neoliberal social imperative of self-enhancement? Combining my criticism of the neoliberal understanding of the body as both designable object and identity project, with my choreographic interest in discovering more of the body's potential, I developed this thesis from the basis of the following thought experiment: If in the Western neoliberal middle class society, the process of creating the individual body usually serves the purpose of achieving a better version of the same self[44], would it then, instead and quite by contrast, not be possible to use the potential openness of the body with a different aim in mind, namely the aim of enabling a process of becoming unfamiliar or even to alienate from one's own self? Thus, my proposition of "becoming unfamiliar to one's own self" is meant to be understood as a possible counter proposal to the social demands of controlling and enhancing bodies, demands that usually aim at enhancing what is similar or even exactly alike while, by the same token, avoiding and even suppressing the unfamiliar and the other.

Accordingly, I followed two specific ideas within my research process. The first idea was researching on choreographic strategies of creating unfamiliar body images with which the members of the research group[45] did not identify. In this context, I considered becoming other, becoming unfamiliar, as a strategy to expand the known range of the individual body- and self-perceptions and to locate the other or the unfamiliar inside the own body. This research on the body as a medium and place for becoming the other, the unfamiliar or the not yet known, was not connected to a pre-defined goal, but rather to an interest in creating temporal states of irritation. Following Waldenfels, who assumes that the experience of the unfamiliar not only implies that we encounter something we do not know yet; rather, the experience of the unfamiliar culminates in the alienation of the experience itself[46], I was interested in the ques-

---

44 Cf. Villa (2008b), p. 264f.
45 I invited the following artists as co-researchers to my artistic research process: Sophie Aigner, Juli Reinartz, Johanna Roggan & Vania Rovisco. For detailed information on their particular role in the research process see chapter 2 On Methods, p. 55ff.
46 Cf. Waldenfels, Bernhard (2006) Grundmotive einer Phänomenologie des Fremden, p. 120.

tion of what the benefit of experiencing the own body and self in ways yet unknown could be.

The second idea was focusing on the notion of play as a potential counter strategy to the neoliberal focus on a goal-oriented work on one's own self. While neoliberal practices of forming and manipulating the body are based on already known procedures with more or less defined rules, in the context of my research, I followed Friedrich Schiller's understanding of play as a mental and/or physical activity which is neither subjectively or objectively contingent, and yet imposes neither inward nor outward necessity.[47] In Schiller's understanding of play, the individual's nature consists of a sensuous part and an intelligible part, which can mutually act and react upon each other. Play is the third force, which is capable of combining both forces and enabling a playful interaction between the sensuous and the intelligible part of the individual. In this particular understanding, play is considered as an "inner-subjective ability to play with one's own cognitive powers".[48]

Thus, in the context of this work, I assumed that play creates a temporally limited experience of freedom for the individual to actively alter its own perception by playing with its way of thinking, and, vice versa, alter its way of thinking by playing with its way of perceiving things. In the particular context of my research, playing with the own perceptions as well as the own thinking of the body became a central strategy of the re-creation of internal and external body images.

Starting from those interests, I developed two artistic research-projects, "the bodies we are" (2016) and "let's face it!" (2017), which I realized as a member of the graduate program "Performing Citizenship"[49]. In the first research project, "the bodies we are", I focused on the following questions: How does the process of consciously creating body images within the choreographic process actually work? What are the limits of this process of creating body images? And: How can the process of creating body images be used as a tool to become unfamiliar to or even alienate from one's own self? In the second research project, "let's face it!", I focused on researching the unfamiliar body images of a body with plenty of faces, a body without a face or a face without a body. This research process was based on the assumption that in the Western culture, the face is a particular part of the body that is often used to recognize and identify

---

47   Cf. Schiller, Friedrich (2014) On the Aesthetic Education of Man, p. 53–67.
48   Cf. Neuenfeld, Jörg (2005) Alles ist Spiel, p. 14.
49   http://performingcitizenship.de/data/en/ (date accessed 5 January 2022)

individuals. Based on this assumption, in "let's face it!", I researched on using masks as a performative practice to let the individual face vanish and to play with non-individual forms of expression.

The specific profile of the graduate program "Performing Citizenship" as a hybrid between artistic and scientific approaches formed the whole research process. My research spanned both practical artistic and theoretical levels. Due to this, my specific research process was conducted in two different contexts. The two artistic research projects took place during several research residencies in dance studios of the institutions K3 | Tanzplan Hamburg at Kampnagel Hamburg, Pact Zollverein Essen, and Tanzfaktur Köln. To these artistic research projects, I invited various co-researchers.[50] The practical experiments I conducted within this group of co-researchers created individual and subjective research experiences from everybody involved. Within the practical research process, those individual and subjective experiences were shared and collected within the research team.

In the theoretical part of my research, I examined different philosophical perspectives on the question of how and where body images are open to change. This theoretical research led to an interest in two philosophical views on the body, very different in their approach to the philosophical perspectives of how bodies are created. One was the phenomenological concept of Maurice Merleau-Ponty with its focus on the body as a perceiving subject, the other one was the constructivist and performative concept of Judith Butler with its focus on how bodies become socially constructed through language. I read both philosophical perspectives with a particular focus: What kind of individual agency can be derived from these theoretical perspectives, regarding my research interest?

In my reading of Merleau-Ponty's phenomenology of the body, I focused on his claim that the body as subject is built through action and perception.[51] In this concept, the body as subject is looked upon as a means of creating a world and as such, of creating everything, including itself, through the partic-

---

50 The co-researchers of the first research project were: Sophie Aigner, Juli Reinartz, Vania Rovisco and Johanna Roggan. The co-researchers of the second research project were: Sophie Aigner and Vania Rovisco. For a more detailed description of the particular co-researchers' roles also compare p. 56.

51 Cf. Merleau-Ponty, Maurice (2012) Phenomenology of Perception .Trans. Donald Landes, p. 95ff.

ular perception of it.⁵² According to Merleau-Ponty, this perception is alterable, depending on how the body is used, since different uses of the body produce different perceptions of the body as well as the surrounding environment. Accordingly, when researching on creating body images with the aim of becoming unfamiliar to one's own self, one idea that derived from this phenomenological concept is to research on strategies to consciously manipulate the way the body is used and perceived.

While reading the constructivist philosopher Judith Butler, I focused on her claim that the body is a linguistic being⁵³ and that its materiality is constructed through language. In her argumentation that the materiality of the body is fully sedimented with social discourses, which all imply particular power structures,⁵⁴ Butler refers to a temporality which is different from the limited timeframe of my artistic research process. Despite that, I considered her idea that bodies are created through processes of description and labeling as very productive when transferring these processes into the practical research. Accordingly, when consciously creating body images with the aim of becoming unfamiliar to one's own self within the choreographic context, one potential strategy that could result from Butler's thinking, is experimenting with processes of creating alternative body labels and descriptions with which to confront the performer's body.

When researching on individual agency, in the process of creating body images within the theoretical context, two more philosophical perspectives were important, which I read as a potential link between Merleau-Ponty and Butler. One was Hegel's thought experiments on the gap between the internal subjective sensory perception and the external objective processes of naming those perceptions.⁵⁵ In his thought experiments, Hegel shows that the internal and subjective perception (of for example a body) must always be different from the external objective act of naming this perception, because firstly the process of naming always happens with a temporal delay, and secondly, by describing something, language translates a subjective individual truth into a universal and objective truth.⁵⁶ While Hegel (in his search for truth) considers this gap

---

52 Cf. Merleau-Ponty (2012), p. 69ff.
53 Cf. Butler (1997) Excitable speech: a politics of the performative, p. 1.
54 Cf. Butler (1997), p. 29.
55 Cf. Hegel, G.W.F. (2003) The Phenomenology of Mind, p. 54ff.
56 Cf. Hegel (2003), p. 59f.

as a dilemma, in the particular context of my research, I considered this gap as a creative potential for consciously recreating and transforming body images.

This creative potential also is an integral part of Schiller's understanding of play.[57] According to Schiller, the individual's capacity of play derives from the understanding that there are two different forces at work inside of an individual – the sensuous impulse (the subjective perception) and the formal impulse (the capacity of reason making, process of naming). Those two impulses, as Schiller states, are simultaneously and mutually subordinated and coordinated, which means that both impulses can act and react upon each other.[58] Therefore, following Schiller, the capacity to play creates a temporally limited experience of freedom to play with one's own cognitive power, since the individual can alter its own perception by consciously altering its way of thinking, and vice versa. Thus, in my particular research process, playing with the own body image includes the conscious transformation of the own perception of body and self.

Throughout my working process, theoretical and practical research on how the body can serve as a place and medium to become unfamiliar to the own self went hand in hand. The present study can be understood as an attempt to make this research process transparent and share the results of both the practical and the theoretical research. Structurally, in this present study, I will continuously change perspectives by alternating chapters dealing with the practical artistic research and chapters concerned with the theoretical research. While the chapters on the practical artistic research focus on the individual subjective experiences of the co-researchers and me as artistic director, the theoretical chapters focus on a rather objective approach.

In chapter 2, I will give a short overview about the current discourse related to my research, referring to three different contexts. Firstly, I will contextualize my individual artistic/scientific research process within the field of artistic research. Secondly, I will draft several sociological perspectives on the body that deal with the body as a medium and place of self-formation and self-optimization. In this context, I will discuss why, from a sociological point of view, the body is not understood as a static, unchangeable entity, but as manipulable and, thus, also negotiable. The here-assembled sociological perspectives on the body address why working on and with the manipulable body can always be understood as working on the self. Based on this, the role that this working

---

57 Cf. Schiller (2014), p. 53–67.
58 Cf. Schiller (2014), p. 54.

on the body and on the self plays in the context of neoliberal society, with its values of self-responsibility and self-optimization, is also addressed.

Thirdly, I will outline various perspectives, both from dance studies and dance practice, that address the notion of a flexible and unfinished body in the contemporary choreographic context. In doing so, I will address the fact that, within the context of contemporary dance, other interests are attached to the work with a negotiable and unfinished body: here, the focus is less on optimization and more on an interest in play and the development of a creative ability to generate temporary body images and physical states with the help of movement and perception.

In chapter 3, I will give a summary of my artistic research method, which could be described as consciously creating gaps between what the body is and what the body is not yet. In order to actively deal with those gaps, I applied different choreographic strategies of appropriation. I thereby consider appropriation as an artistic strategy that includes the intentional borrowing of pre-existing images, objects, and ideas.[59] However, unlike in Pop art[60], where artists use appropriation (of well-known images, objects, and ideas) mostly as a strategy to challenge notions of originality and authorship[61], in the context of my particular research, I consider appropriation as a choreographic strategy to borrow something that is external to the self, with the particular interest in creating encounters with the unfamiliar, the irritating, or the not yet known or accepted.

In chapter 4, I will approach the question of how body images can actively be created from altering philosophical as well as choreographic perspectives. In chapter 4.2, I will discuss Merleau-Ponty's concept of the body as an agent, i.e. as a perceiving subject, to theoretically reflect on the question why body images can be influenced by the particular way, how the individual body is used and perceived. In chapter 4.3, I will switch to the practical artistic research. Here, I will reflect on the practical experiments of the artistic research and focus on the question how unfamiliar body-perceptions can be generated.

In chapter 4.4, I will change perspective and discuss Butler's concept of the body created through processes of labeling. In chapter 4.5, I will reflect on the artistic research experiments with the particular focus on how unfamiliar body

---

59 Cf. https://www.moma.org/learn/moma_learning/glossary/ (date accessed 5 January 2022)
60 Cf. https://remixculture.ca/appropriation-in-pop-art/ (date accessed 5 January 2022)
61 Cf. Appropriation Now! Texte zur Kunst, Heft 46/2002

descriptions can be used as a tool to initiate alternative self- and body perceptions. In chapter 4.6, I will discuss the creative gap between sensory perception and processes of naming by discussing Hegel's thought experiments on sensuous certainty and Schiller's understanding of play. In chapter 4.7, I will bring those theoretical thoughts into a dialogue with the artistic experiments appropriating an unfamiliar method, when researching on the body as a role by applying working strategies of the Method Acting technique.

Based on the experiences and insights gained from the first artistic research project, I will propose to think of the body as a sensitive container in chapter 4.8. With this choreographic working term of a body as a sensitive container, I will try to uncouple the body from the concept of the body as an "identity project".

In order to look more deeply into the topic of the body as a place with which to create and experience self-distancing, I will, in chapter 5 and based on Richard Sennett's findings, present a short historical overview of diverse concepts of the body in different phases of the 18th, 19th and 20th centuries.

In chapter 6, I will deal with my second artistic research project, "Let's face it". The starting point of the second research process was my interest in researching on performative and choreographic strategies that could be used to consciously play with evading and blurring clear forms of identification. Linking this interest with Sennett's request of practicing play in order to repractice self-distancing, I became interested in the human face, since it is the particular body part that, in Western culture, is considered to be the obvious place individuals get recognized and identified by.[62] Based on this interest, my aim for the second artistic research project "Let's face it!" was to develop choreographic and performative strategies that could be used for distancing oneself from one's own individual face.

This research also led to a deeper interest in the topic of the mask. In the context of my research, I considered the mask as a means for simultaneously hiding and showing oneself, a medium that can be used to playfully transform into another being and temporarily disappear as an identifiable subject.[63] This playful process of letting the own recognizable face disappear, also provoked alternative imaginations and fantasies about the own body and self.

My research on the mask as a performative and choreographic strategy for creating bodies with plenty of faces, bodies with no face or, alternatively, faces

---

62   For a history of the face cf. Belting, Hans (2014) Faces. Eine Geschichte des Gesichts.
63   Cf. Brauneck, Manfred (2020) Masken – Theater, Kult und Brauchtum, p. 9.

without bodies made it possible to artistically construct a very particular form of body, a non-permanent body that consciously played with the construction, de-construction, and re-construction of diverse temporal body images, such as those of a plant, a leaking hole, a surveillance camera, or a warrior. Thus, the research process "Let's face it!" examined the boundaries between identification and alienation, between subject and object, between having a face and not having a face.

I will end this thesis with a reflection on the utopian potential of the results found. The questions I will discuss are: In what way might those strategies of playing with self-distancing, of considering the own body as something other than an identity project, be of inspiration when trying to emancipate the body from the neoliberal social imperative of self-optimization and control? To what extent might the insights of the practical research projects inspire a change in attitude towards the body in the actual neoliberal social culture of self-optimization?

2. State of the Art

This paper is the written part of my Ph.D. thesis which, throughout, combines an artistic and a scientific approach. It was developed within the academic framework of the post-graduate program called "Performing Citizenship: New articulations of urban citizenship in 21st century metropolis"[1]. As one of only a few such post-graduate programs in Germany, it facilitated artistic research projects embedded in an academic context[2] and connected to participatory practices. To contextualize this paper with regard to the field of artistic research, I will outline a few particularities and challenges potentially arising in this field.

In Germany, artistic research is a relatively recent field, which has been practiced and widely discussed within its particular contemporary choreographic contexts since the nineteen-nineties.[3] In the context of artistic research, choreographic work is not primarily considered as a tool for achieving the result of a production. On the contrary, a shift of focus can be observed, leading away from the final artistic product and towards the creative process itself.[4] In this context, the creative process, in which artists focus on investi-

---

1   The graduate school was supported by a cooperation of the HafenCity Universität (HCU)/department of Metropolitan Culture, by the Hochschule für Angewandte Wissenschaft Design (HAW), and by two non-academic cultural institutions, the FUNDUS THEATER and K3 – Center for Choreography | Tanzplan Hamburg.
2   http://performingcitizenship.de/data/en/category/forschungsprojekte/ (date accessed 5 January 2022)
3   For overview of those different debates cf. for example: Kleinschmidt, Katharina (2018) Künstlerische Forschung als Wissensgefüge. Eine Praxeologie des Probens, p. 20–34.
4   Cf. Haarmann, Anke (2019) Artistic Research. Eine epistemologische Ästhetik, p. 16.

gating different topics or questions in their artistic practice, is often described as a 'laboratory'[5].

One central question in different debates on artistic research is what kind of knowledge it produces.[6] This discussion started due to the observation that artistic research is actually happening in the frame of the individual artistic practice. For that reason, the resulting specific knowledge is mostly considered to be individual knowledge based on the particular artist's subjective experiences.[7] Since it is common for artistic research projects to be interdisciplinary, combining different fields of art or oscillating between theory and practice, artistic researchers often leave the grounds of their own expertise and move toward areas of 'not knowing'[8]. In this context, it is usually claimed that artistic practice as an experimental form of research expands its own boundaries.[9]

Due to the Bologna Reform in 1999, artistic research has been recognized as an academic discipline, which made it possible to carry out artistic research projects

within the frame of an academic thesis. In contrast to other European countries, such as Sweden, Norway, or Great Britain, for example, German art academies or universities do not allow for artistic Ph.D. projects to research

---

5   Cf. Peters, Sibylle (2011) Der Vortrag als Performance. Or also: Cf. Stamer, Peter (2015) Was ist ein künstlerisches Labor? In: Gehm, Sabine; Husemann, Pirkko; von Wilcke, Katharina (eds.) Wissen in Bewegung. p 64.
6   Cf. Haarmann (2019), p. 33.
7   This is why in the debate on artistic research the created knowledge is often labeled as "other knowledge" or "dynamic", "physical" or "implicit knowledge" which is different from rational knowledge linked to reason. Yet dance scientist Katharina Kleinschmidt, in her thesis "Künstlerische Forschung als Wissensgefüge", argues against this claimed binary of artistic knowledge (as other knowledge) versus scientific knowledge (as rational, linked to reason). According to Kleinschmidt, in this binary thinking, art as such is considered to be the unspeakable and is thus set against the sciences, which are automatically associated with operating through argumentation, clear-cut terms, and definitions. Kleinschmidt claims that, when looking at the matter from this perspective, one systematically neglects the analytical efforts of artistic research, efforts that consist in discussions, the verbalizing of aesthetic experiences, in feedback processes and in the forming of definitions, all of which make up a vital part of choreographic research processes. Cf. Kleinschmidt (2018), p. 17.
8   Cf. Borgdorff, Henk (2010) Artistic Research as Boundary Work. In: Caduff, Corina; Siegenthaler, Fiona; Wälchli, Tan (eds.) Art and Artistic Research.
9   Cf. Slager, Henk (2009) Art and Method. In: Elkins, James (ed.) Artists with Ph.Ds. On the New Doctoral Degree in Studio Art, p. 51.

exclusively in the field of art. In Germany, doing artistic research is explicitly defined as trans-disciplinary, i.e. as including the artistic as well as the scientific field. This is how the post-graduate program "Performing Citizenship" defined it, too.[10]

The institutionalization of artistic research made it possible to realize artistic research projects not only in the context of artistic production, but also within an academic framework. Parallel to this institutionalization, a controversial debate on the differences between artistic research and academic research emerged. In the context of this debate, an intensive discussion has been taking place on the specific methods, research designs and the transparency of knowledge production of artistic research.[11] At the heart of the debate lies the question whether artistic research – with its subjective and intuitive character – can be qualified as research and, if so, what methodical standards are needed to qualify it.

A compromise in this debate has been suggested by philosopher Anke Haarmann in her book "Artistic Research"[12]. Haarmann points out the danger that, with the field of artistic research still being so young, unsuitable methodological standards will be expected of artistic research, unsuitable or even counterproductive due to the lack of historical experience in this field and the lack of epistemic expertise.[13] As an alternative to adapting goal-oriented and regulatory scientific methods, Haarmann proposes pursuing what she calls a "nachdenkliche Methodologie" (reflective methodology)[14]. Such an approach, according to Haarmann, does not deny that the actual process of artistic research is subjective and intuitive, but at the same time, through a reflection of the process, it offers transparency and comprehensibility with regard to the actual individual decisions taken within the research.

In her particular methodological approach, Haarmann ascribes a vital role to imagination – which she defines as inventive as well as exploratory.[15] Based on the thoughts of performers Victoria Peréz Royo, José A. Sánchez,

---

10   The 'Graduate School' of Universität der Künste Berlin can be distinguished from this perspective. The program does not define artistic research as artistic-scientific, however it does not provide an academic Ph.D.
11   Cf. for example: Caduff, Corina; Siegenthaler, Fiona; Wälchli, Tan (eds.) Art and Artistic Research. But also: Kleinschmidt, Katharina (2018), p. 20–33.
12   Haarmann, Anke (2019)
13   Cf. Haarmann (2019), p. 284.
14   Cf. Haarmann (2019), p. 287.
15   Cf. Haarmann (2019), p. 289f.

and Christina Blanco[16], Haarmann defines imagination in two ways: as a tool for deconstructing, juggling, and reconstructing existing connections.; and as an aesthetic means of gaining insight into alternative realities and ways of transforming reality through artistic work. Here, artistic comprehension goes hand in hand with artistic practice. This is why Haarmann suggests labeling the outcome of this process not as knowledge, but as "Einsicht" (insight).[17]

The notion of 'insight' as the result of artistic research processes points to the fact that artistic research only rarely aims at generating objective data. On the contrary, the term 'insight' emphasizes the character of an individual and negotiable proposal, a proposal that means to actually represent the particular way of seeing, showing, and performing that is inherent to artistic practice.[18] It is in this sense that Haarmann claims that artistic research can also be considered as a space for action and negotiation in which alternative cultural or sociological realities can develop.

This paper is meant to represent such a space for negotiation – a space in which, through artistic practice as well as theoretical discussion, I seek to imagine, try out, and propose alternative perspectives on bodies not subjected to optimization and control. In this context, I do not consider practical and theoretical research to be opposites, but, on the contrary, as different perspectives that will inspire, complement, and question each other during the process.

In how far does this transdisciplinary ground of research – between theory and practice – have an impact on the contextualization of my work? Concerning the "State of the art" of this thesis I would like to point out three difficulties or challenges that I encountered while locating my particular research within a wider context. Those challenges are what, in my view, distinguishes a purely scientific Ph.D. thesis. 1. Since the field of artistic academic research has not been in existence for long, only few results of artistic-scientific work(s) have been published so far. Therefore, it is difficult to contextualize this thesis within a pool of already existing artistic research projects[19], a method normally inherent to academic work. 2. My interdisciplinary approach, alternating between

---

16 Cf. Peréz Royo, Victoria; Sánchez, José A.; Blanco, Christina: In-definitions. Forschung in den performativen Künsten. In: Peters, Sibylle (2013) Das Forschen Aller. Artistic Research als Wissensproduktion zwischen Kunst, Wissenschaft und Gesellschaft, p. 23–46.

17 Cf. Haarmann (2019), p. 45.

18 Cf. Haarmann (2019), p. 29.

19 One example of contextualizing artistic research programs is the online resource "Participatory Art based research" (PABR). PABR understands research first and fore-

theory and practice, led me into various fields of knowledge in philosophy, sociology, and dance science without me actually being an academic in those fields. My specific handling of the theoretical texts was guided by my interest in making those theoretical fields productive for my artistic research process. 3. In scientific research, the first step is to find a topic that has not been well researched yet. However, this was not how I started my own research process. In fact, the starting point of my research project was a combination of a subjective observation about society and an individual artistic interest. Neither sought to fill a gap in (academic) research. I rather worked 'backwards', quite in line with Haarmann's definition, in the sense that I first carried out my artistic research project and in the research process related it to current academic and artistic discourses.[20]

My interdisciplinary approach oscillating between theory and practice has touched upon sociological debates just as well as debates on the science and the practice of dance – all a result of the central question of my research of how, in the Western neoliberal society, the body could be disentangled from the present social requirements of self-optimization and self-control.

The "State of the Art" presented here therefore consists of two parts. In the first part I will outline various sociological perspectives that focus on the body as a medium and a place for self-formation and self-optimization. Here I will look into why, from a sociological standpoint, the body is not defined as a static, unchangeable entity, but as something that is open to transformation and change, and in consequence which is considered to be negotiable. These sociological perspectives on the body show that working on and with the manipulable body can always, simultaneously, be considered as work on the self.

In the second part of my "State of the art" I will outline various perspectives on dance science and dance practice that focus on the notion of a flexible and unfinished body in the present choreographic context. I will show that, in the context of contemporary dance, the expectations and interests linked to the work with and on a negotiable, unfinished body are quite different. The focus here is not so much on an interest in optimization, but rather on an interest in playing and, with the help of movement and perception, developing the creative ability to generate temporary body images and physical states.

---

20   most as a triangular relation and interaction between art, science and society. Cf.: https://pab-research.de
Also cf. https://pab-research.de/research-map/ (date accessed 5 January 2022)

2.1 Sociological perspectives on the body as a medium and place for self-formation

Physical perception and sensing as the base of forming the self

In his book "Leib, Körper, Identität"[21], sociologist Robert Gugutzer attributes a central role in the formation and creation of the own self and the own identity to the body. The starting point of his deliberations is Helmuth Plessner's differentiation between "Leibsein" (being a body) and "Körperhaben" (having a body)[22]. As Gugutzer states, Plessner's term of "Leibsein" refers to the biological, organic human existence that is made up of limbs, torso, organs of perception, etc. Therefore the notion of "Leibsein" is connected with the idea of the body as a perceiving subject.

"Körperhaben", on the other hand, refers to the body seen as an object which the 'owner' of that body has conscious access to and can actively use in an instrumental as well as expressive way. According to Gugutzer, "Körperhaben" represents a lifelong (learning) task, which is continuously influenced by processes of socialization.[23] In his view, the ability to consciously perceive one's own body as an object that can actively be made use of leads to the possibility of perceiving the body as negotiable, malleable, and even optimizable.[24] This particular ability forms the precondition to a human being developing a 'self', an 'I'.[25] It is precisely this double aspect in the human condition that, according to Gugutzer, confronts the human individual with the task to search and establish an identity and self, since it confronts the individual with the question of who it is and who it wants to be.[26]

Gugutzer defines the human 'self' as a unity of "Leibsein", i.e. the body's perceiving and sensitive dimension, and of "Körperhaben", i.e. the body's reflecting dimension.[27] Therefore, Gugutzer concludes that the forming of a self and of an identity is always connected to the body as such. Concerning the formation of a self and of an identity, Gugutzer focuses in particular on the body's inner perspective, considering perceiving, sensing, and experiencing as

---

21 Cf. Gugutzer (2002)
22 Cf. Gugutzer (2002), p. 124f.
23 Cf. Gugutzer (2002), p. 66.
24 Cf. Gugutzer (2015), p. 45.
25 Cf. Gugutzer (2002), p. 65.
26 Cf. Gugutzer (2002), p. 68.
27 Cf. Gugutzer (2002), p. 67.

the base for forming the own self and identity.²⁸ Referring to Merleau-Ponty's and Schmitz's phenomenological thinking, Gugutzer argues that physical experiences form the pre-verbal basis of language and thinking.²⁹ Consequently, Gugutzer claims that reflection is always preceded by and based on actual physical experiences.

The forming of an identity and of the self, therefore, is the result of an interplay between physical experience and language-based processes of active reflection, with Gugutzer defining identity as the preliminary result of physical experiences that are potentially subject to change. Gugutzer claims that physical experiences need, with the help of self-narration, to be integrated into a convincing, consistent physical body biography, with identity possibly being defined as the production of a coherent subjective perception. Being identical with oneself therefore means actually feeling identical with oneself.³⁰

The body as carrier and representative of social roles

The sociologist Erving Goffman describes an external social perspective on the body as a medium for self- and identity formation. In his book "The presentation of self in everyday life³¹", Goffman considers the social world to be a theatrical performance, in which the acting individuals use their bodies to represent different social roles. According to Goffman, each of those social roles is linked to a particular social status, to specific rights and duties, and to implicit physical norms.³² Therefore, Goffman does not claim that self- and identity formation via the body are a result of an individual's physical sensations. On the contrary, Goffman demonstrates how the body's availability as a tool for self- and identity formation is actually used as a medium for self-presentation. In Goffman's view, having the body available as tool is used to fulfill specific patterns of acting in social communication and to create a complex impression that is implicitly linked to that particular social role.

Goffman points out that during one's self-presentation in front of vis-à-vis others, sometimes also problems occur that make it necessary to employ certain techniques, such as putting up a façade, polishing one's image, or creating

---

28   Cf. Gugutzer (2002), p. 74.
29   Cf. Gugutzer (2002), p. 139.
30   Cf. Gugutzer (2002), p. 130.
31   Cf. Goffman, Erving (1959) The Presentation of Self in Everyday Life.
32   Cf. Goffman (1959), p. 15f.

a fake appearance, for example.³³ When such techniques are employed in social interaction, the body is deliberately stage-managed through conscious use of body language, posture, facial expression, dress, etc. The aim of those techniques is to achieve specific conscious effects with the help of the body that in turn will contribute to the performance of one's own social role.³⁴ According to Goffman, the expressive use of one's own body as an object and a tool is not primarily the result of an individual decision, but rather is determined by inherent social roles.

The body as effect of the power of discourse

In discourse analysis, perspectives on the body are often based on the theories of philosopher and historian Michel Foucault, who thinks the body as a construct of an apparatus, i.e., an intertwining of discourses, practices, and institutions.³⁵ From the perspective of discourse analysis bodies are constructed by what is actually said about them in scientific as well as sociological discourse, as in that discourse specific body norms, body images, and body techniques³⁶ are constructed that, in turn have an effect on the bodies of the particular society of that time.

From this angle, discourse always exercises power over bodies. They do so by establishing rules that define what is included and what is excluded so that the "other/alien", the "strange", and the "deviation" become unacceptable as potential alternatives or are automatically subjected to modification, in people's minds as well as in social reality.³⁷ The specific power exercised here, according to Foucault, does not act as a visible sovereign power, but as a specific framework of relations, as a 'bio-power', a 'somatic power'³⁸ that determines the individuals' behavior and thus has an effect on their bodies.

In post-disciplinary societies that affirm self-government, bio-power therefore does not act as a superior law enforced from above, but makes the

---

33   Cf. Goffmann (1959), p. 22ff.
34   Cf. Goffmann (1959), p. 1.
35   Cf. Bublitz, Hannelore (2017) Diskurstheorie. In: Gugutzer, Robert; Klein, Gabriele; Meuser, Michael (eds). Handbuch der Körpersoziologie, p. 190.
36   Body techniques are physical activities such as walking, running, swimming, digging, etc. that are performed in a particular way specific to the society the individual is situated in. Also cf. Mauss, Marcel (2010) Soziologie und Anthropologie. Band 2, p. 202.
37   Cf. Bublitz (2017), p. 191.
38   Cf. Foucault, Michel (1978) Dispositive der Macht. Über Sexualität, Wissen und Wahrheit, p. 109.

individuals subject themselves to the socially accepted physical norms of their time through self-discipline and self-care. Here, according to Foucault, technologies of the self are applied that tie in with the topic of "taking care of oneself"[39]. Those technologies of the self enable the individual to carry out, as a result of one's own effort or with the help of others, a number of operations on one's own body or soul, and on one's own way of thinking and behaving.[40]

The philosopher Judith Butler builds on Foucault's discourse analysis and widens it by adding her concept of performativity[41]. In her concept of performativity she emphasizes the specific power of language to produce effects and claims that the individual's identity and body must be constructed through performative acts. Based on Foucault's thinking, Butler assumes that verbal descriptions of bodies always automatically imply specific physical categories, ascriptions, and norms that are socially determined. According to Butler, labeling bodies through constantly repeated linguistic ascriptions creates a specific effect on those bodies.[42] The reason for this, Butler claims, is that the individual then adopts, internalizes, and visibly embodies the expectations and ascriptions immanent to the language used, which in turn results in the construction of a subject and an identity.[43] Butler therefore considers performativity as a strategy for creating a subject, viewing the body as the place and medium for the construction of a self.[44]

The body as the place of hard work on the optimizable self

Based on Foucault's and Butler's theories, sociologist Paula Irene Villa researches how the embodiment of social norms through bodily self-techniques becomes visible in the everyday life of Western neoliberal society. According to Villa, in the present neoliberal society, the range of physical strategies used for conscious work on the individual self spans from unobtrusive practices such as hygiene, dress code, clothing, or 'healthy food' to conscious projects such as dieting, body forming via sports, manifold therapies in the grey zone between health, wellness, and optimization (vitamin cures, massages, fasting,

---

39   Cf. Foucault, Michel (1988) The Care of the Self.
40   Foucault, Michel (1993) Technologien des Selbst. In: Gutman, Huck; Hutton, Patrick H.; Martin, Luther H. (eds.) Technologien des Selbst, p. 26.
41   Cf. Butler, Judith (1991) Das Unbehagen der Geschlechter, p. 206.
42   Cf. Butler, Judith (1991), p. 58.
43   Cf. Butler, Judith (1993) Bodies That Matter, p. 32.
44   Cf. Butler (1991), p. 206.

etc.), and even manipulation of the body through plastic surgery or gene therapy.[45] According to Villa, the conscious work on the body is always marked by ambivalence, since it simultaneously comprises the potential for creative self-empowerment as well as extreme submission to social norms.[46]

Referring to sociologist Ulrich Böckling's concept of the "unternehmerisches Selbst" (the entrepreneurial self)[47], Villa claims that the body in present Western society has become 'raw material' for self-design, meeting with a constant imperative to work on the individual physical self-optimization. In this concept, working on the own body is understood as an attempt for increasing the individual value. Referring to Böckling, Villa states that individuals who do not aim at optimization, who are not constantly working (and working hard) at improving their body and thus, their self, do not deserve social recognition.[48] Only subjects acting like entrepreneurs still qualify for recognition. Against this background, the somatic technologies of the self can, according to Villa, also be read as an attempt at ensuring reliability in the context of an increasingly uncertain post-modern social environment.[49] Gugutzer also addresses this aspect by making the case that the body, because it is constantly available, is particularly suitable to the task of creating reliability.[50]

According to Villa, in self-techniques like aesthetic plastic surgery, social, ethical, and political questions are automatically dealt with. Villa claims that those questions finally converge on the core question of what individuals actually can, may, and must do with their bodies – in other words, how, in the present society, individuals deal with the social nature of having a body.[51] In Villa's view, it is in particular the women's rights movement of the 1960s that tried to create self-empowerment via the body as such by actually making visible bodies that did not meet the norms, and by looking upon the body as a living place for alternative possibilities.[52] This feminist self-determination and self-empowerment through a conscious objectification of one's own body inadvertently paved the way, Villa states, for the concept of "worrying about oneself" (in Foucault's sense) and it has led to women changing into clients of health

---

45   Cf. Villa (2008a), p. 10.
46   Cf. Villa (2008), p. 8.
47   Bröckling, Ulrich (2007)
48   Cf. Villa (2008a), p. 12.
49   Cf. Villa (2013), p. 59.
50   Cf.Villa (2013), p. 59.
51   Cf. Villa (2008b), p. 251f.
52   Cf. Villa (2013), p. 68.

services, for example, today subjecting themselves to permanent self-observation, self-control, and self-optimization.[53]

In Villa's view, a culmination in this culture of self-optimization becomes evident in various TV casting formats[54] that stage the work on the own body as a chance to achieve a better and more self-determined life. While the women's movement referred to a concept of normality based on the obvious variety in actually existing (female) bodies, the TV shows Villa has analyzed follow a different reference point. As Villa states, those media formats, as well as plastic surgery, or several fitness apps promote an imaginary, ideological norm that individual subjects are expected to arrive at as autonomously as possible through imitation.

In opposition to her analysis of contemporary somatic technologies of the self, Villa also emphasizes their general potential for resilience and creativity. Here, she argues that individuals will always find ways to live with particular discourses without being destroyed by them[55]. It is in this sense that Villa claims, that somatic self-techniques always comprise the potential to develop alternative desires, hopes, and ideas with regard to one's own body, all of which may in turn contribute to the development of alternative discourses.[56] According to Villa, this self-empowerment is taking place in queer and feminist contexts, for example, in which various forms of "reclaiming" one's own body – also with the help of aesthetic surgery – are employed in order to express one's individual empowerment.[57] This phenomenon of self-empowerment can also be observed in the "body positivity" movement, for example, which is fighting for the abolition of unrealistic and discriminating beauty ideals, and engaging for diversity and social justice.[58]

Sociologist Anke Abraham dedicates her research to the various difficulties that occur in the context of the present capitalist neoliberal society,

---

53   Cf. Villa (2008b), p. 259.
54   such as: "The Swan", "Germany's next top model".
55   Cf. Villa (2008b), p. 267.
56   An example for this is the recent diversity discourse. Cf. for example: Rees, Anuschka (2019) Beyond Beautiful.
57   Cf. for example Preciado, Paul Beatriz (2013) Testo Junkie. Sex, Drugs and Biopolitics in the Pharmacopornographic Era.
58   Cf. for example Cwynar-Horta, Jessica: The Commodification of the Body Positive Movement on Instagram. In: Stream: Inspiring Critical Thought. 8, Nr.2, 2016, p. 36–56.

when searching for a more appreciative attitude toward the body.[59] According to Abraham, this alternative attitude is impeded by the following principles inherent in neoliberal society, namely accumulation of capital, competition, and increase in performance. Abraham claims that it is exactly those principles that lead to a certain way of treating the own body, unhealthily suppressing physical needs (i.e., for regeneration, leisure time, physical activity, genuine balance) on the one hand, and asking for constant body optimization on the other.[60] In this context, Abraham concludes that the idea of the human body's constant availability and malleability is closely linked to the social request of expanding individual boundaries in order to persist in social competition.

When individuals compare themselves with the widespread body images produced and promoted by the media, and then fail to meet the implicitly set physical standards, they will suffer, since they will perceive their own bodies as deficient.[61] Thus, as Abraham points out, what begins as a simple option of change later turned into a necessity to change, even an enforcement of change, pressuring the individual to utilize the suitable products and services provided for self-optimization. Abraham describes this process of change as gradual, but with massive consequences for the individual's integrity.[62]

To escape from this particular cultural pattern of thinking and acting, according to Abraham, new ways of thinking are necessary.[63] Abraham's practical suggestion on this remains relatively vague, though. She proposes respecting the body as a "miracle" and to search for opportunities of practical experience through which the potential of this miracle becomes perceptible.[64]

Forming the self as a chance for self-empowerment

Based on the sociological observation that, in our post-industrial meritocracy, an increasing number of individuals are confronted with a normative expectation to continuously reinvent, adapt, and optimize[65] themselves, sociologist Thomas Alkemeyer raises the question of what kind of agency could be attributed to individuals under these particular social conditions.[66] Similar to

---

59   Cf. Abraham (2010), p. 113.
60   Cf. Abraham/Müller (2010), p. 20.
61   Cf. Abraham (2010), p. 125.
62   Cf. Abraham (2010), p. 126f.
63   Cf. Abraham/Müller (2010), p. 21.
64   Cf. Abraham (2010), p. 131.
65   Cf. for example Reckwitz, Andreas (2017) The Invention of Creativity
66   Cf. Alkemeyer/Budde/Freist (2013), p. 21.

Villa and Abraham, Alkemeyer, too, picks out body forming and optimization as crucial self-techniques, used especially in aspiring middle class milieus to achieve a holistic self-formation. Here, according to Alkemeyer, the body in its perfected form appears as a kind of protective armor against undesired physical phenomena such as age, illness, inefficiency, slackening, etc.[67]

Investigating the question of how individuals can meet social expectations for flexibility, self-optimization, and self-management in an active and self-determined way, Alkemeyer proposes a praxeological perspective on the subject.[68] Here, the body is not looked upon as a representative of an ideal self, but is observed as a medium and a place for becoming a subject. Like approaches from discourse analysis, Alkemeyer's thoughts are based on the assumption that bodies move in social fields which are pre-determined by cultural conventions.

However, when employing the term "Selbst-Bildung"[69] (self-formation), Alkemeyer explicitly focuses on the individual agency. He claims that, in this sense, self-formation is a physical process of discovery, invention, and creation that takes place within a particular sociocultural context.[70] This performative understanding of a subject differs from a modern idea of an autonomous subject as well as from approaches in discourse analysis that reduce the acting individuals to mere agents of external social structures.[71] When directly applied to the idea of the body's potential emancipation from the social request for self-optimization, the term of "Selbst-Bildung" (self-formation) instigates the following question: How can physical processes of discovering, inventing, and creating that do not primarily aim at optimization and control be fostered?

The sociological perspectives by Villa, Abraham, and Alkmeyer, in particular, focus on a critical analysis of the body's specific role within the present, neoliberal meritocratic society. What links their perspectives is a common interest in alternative spaces within the social context described above – alternative spaces for handling the social request for optimization of body and self. When it comes to practical suggestions, however, all three authors remain relatively vague. Villa and Abraham in particular make it clear that the principle

---

67 Cf. Alkemeyer/Budde/Freist (2013), p. 13.
68 Cf. Alkemeyer/Budde/Freist (2013), p. 19.
69 Cf. Alkemeyer/Budde/Freist (2013), p. 21.
70 Cf. Alkemeyer/Budde/Freist (2013), p. 21.
71 Cf. Alkemeyer/Budde/Freist (2013), p. 26.

of optimization leads to a very specific way of handling the body, mostly connected to more or less hard work on the body.

The question of emancipation from the social demand for self-optimization therefore also leads to the question of possible alternatives to this WORK on the body. It is precisely this question from which my practical artistic research process started from. While the sociological perspectives outlined above focus on a critical analysis of a status quo, in my research process I used the choreographic field to imagine and rehearse alternative ways of using and reflecting on bodies.

2.2 Self-formation in contemporary dance practice and choreography

The reason why the choreographic field suits itself well to create alternative discourse on the body, in my view, also derives from the particular understanding of the body in the contemporary dance context. As a highly heterogeneous art field, contemporary dance provides a wide variety of practices[72] and techniques to form the body. In this subchapter, I will outline different insights into the educational dance context as well as into the choreographic context, in order to show that in the contemporary dance context, the interest lies less on working on the body, but on discovering and inventing (yet unknown) potentials of the body.

Self-formation in contemporary dance education and training

Looking at contemporary dance training and education, one can find a huge variety of different movement practices and techniques. They range from release-based techniques to modern and ballet techniques as well as somatic practices such as Body-Mind-Centering, Feldenkrais, Alexander-technique, or Klein-technique[73]. Since contemporary dancers train themselves in such a

---

72 In the context of this thesis, I define "practice" as physical practice that prefigures a physical action, but does not determine it. This means that a "practice" (as opposed to a technique) offers the dancer a wider space for acting individually. See also Alkemeyer (2013), p. 47. In contrast to 'practice', I consider 'technique' to be a physical method with clearly defined rules, thus limiting the space for individual agency.

73 Also cf. p. 17 of this paper

variety of different practices and techniques, the dance scientist Susan Foster states that the "selves" of contemporary dancers are aesthetically unspecific and highly flexible.[74] In addition to Foster, in my opinion, it is not only this way of working that enables contemporary dancers to develop highly flexible notions of their own selves, but also – especially – the somatic understanding of the body that leads to a particular openness with which dancers can learn how to actively and consciously experiment with altering their own body- and self-perception.

Based on the phenomenological concept of Leibsein und Körperhaben[75] somatic practices consider the body to be a unity of body and mind[76]. This particular understanding of the body becomes apparent in terms like "mindful body"/"embodied mind"[77] that are often used in this field. What in my opinion is striking about somatic practices, such as Body Mind Centering or Feldenkrais is that mind and body are considered as tools with which to actively and consciously affect, influence, and manipulate each other.[78]

Many contemporary dance trainings based on this somatic understanding of the body, such as the practice Minding Motion by Gill Glarke[79] or the Gaga technique[80] by Ohad Naharin, for example, are primarily interested in exploring the individual movement potentials of the body. Within this process, somatic practices combine two different layers: They create physical and perceptual experiences through movement and touching and they reflect on those experiences on a verbal and discursive level. Both layers combined aim at enlarging the dancer's individual awareness of the body.

The practice Minding Motion, for example, uses different tools to foster attention and awareness of the body, such as sharing anatomical images, creating complex imaginations by using language or hands-on work. What is strik-

---

74 Cf. Foster (2006), p. 241.
75 Also cf. p. 34f. of this paper
76 Cf. for example Diehl/Lampert (eds.) (2011) p. 206. In this understanding the body is not understood separate from the mind. This understanding/conception of the body is also linked with more recent discourse in cognitive science. Cf. for example Noe, Alva (2006) Action in Perception.
77 Cf. Clarke, Gill; Cramer, Franz Anton; Müller, Gisela (2011) Gill Clarke – Minding Motion. In: Diehl, Ingo & Lampert, Friederike (ed) (2011) Dance Techniques 2010 – Tanzplan Deutschland, p. 204.
78 Cf. Clarke/Cramer/Müller (2011), p. 201.
79 Cf. Diehl/Lampert (2011), p. 200–229.
80 Cf. https://www.gagapeople.com/ (date accessed 5 January 2022)

ing in Clarke's approach and what, in my opinion, is typical of dance practices based on a somatic understanding of the body, is the specific role of language. When exploring, for example, the movement possibilities of the pelvis area, Clarke combines a verbal anatomical explanation and functional analysis of the pelvis area with a rather metaphorical language.[81] By describing this body part as a "bowl", Clarke aims at encouraging an immediate visualization, which in turn affects and potentially alters the internal body image of the dancers. This change in the internal body image potentially leads to a change in the internal perception of that body. In this case, it enables the dancers to become aware, for example, of the dynamic volume and the three-dimensionality of the pelvis while they are moving. Accordingly, this creation of an alternative body image of the pelvis, in turn fosters alternative ways of moving from and with the pelvis.

In this context, language is not only used in an explanatory, but also in a figurative and suggestive way. It facilitates rather than instructs movement.[82] Through her particular use of language in combination with the physical and perceptual experiences of the dancers, Clarke initiates a temporary shift of their internal body image, which leads to the dancers' experience of alternative movement- and self-perceptions. On the other hand, language also plays an important role when reflecting on the dancers' physical experiences.[83] In the practice of "talking through"[84], dancers learn to transform their individual physical experiences and physical perceptions which they had while they were moving back into language. In this translation, new descriptions and terms can potentially be found and shared in the group, too.

As a conclusion, one can say that what dancers learn in this particular somatic approach to the body, is rather not to apply fixed movement techniques but to develop their own creativity in playing and experimenting with alternative movement and perception potentials, as well as generating alternative ways of describing and labeling the body. In this context, the mindful body can be considered as a laboratory from which new observations arise, and ideas

---

81 Cf. Clarke/Cramer/Müller (2011), p. 224.
82 Cf. Clarke/Cramer/Müller (2011), p. 217.
83 In chapter 4.4. and 4.5. of this paper, I will discuss the use of language to reflect on the physical experience in relation to Judith Butler's claim of the body as a linguistic being.
84 Cf. Clarke/Cramer/Müller (2011), p. 216.

and images are played out and tested.[85] In this context the body image is nothing stable, but something that is always open to potential changes.

Minding Motion as a movement practice is primarily interested in reaching a state of ease, efficiency, and freedom in the functional movement of the body[86]. On the other hand, the movement practice also teaches dancers to use the own body as a field for individual exploration. In my opinion, this particular approach to the body as a laboratory where movement potentials can be explored is a prerequisite for using the body as a medium and place for individual research on artistic and social questions.

Closely connected with the understanding of the body as laboratory is the format of "movement-research" which plays an important role for generating and exploring movement possibilities in both contemporary dance trainings and in choreographic processes. In this context, movement research is mostly understood as improvisation guided by tasks that are also referred to as scores.[87] Tasks and constraints can be understood as a specific framing that enables dancers not only to reproduce their usual movement habits, but to discover and generate unknown or surprising movement qualities, patterns of movements, and/or perceptions of the body.

Comparing this work on and with the body in the contemporary dance context, with the neoliberal self-techniques aiming at body optimization and enhancement that I have discussed above, it becomes evident that in the present contemporary dance context, work on and with the body is connected less to measurable standards, norms or ideals but that here the emphasis is on the playful process of exploring. This way, this specific work on and with the body mainly consists in the uncovering of the body's potentials, with those potentials definitely not being defined in advance.[88] In comparison with body work that aims at self-optimization according to society's expectations, yet another difference can be noticed: The body work aiming at optimization through dieting, sports, or plastic surgery often interferes radically with the physical materiality, aiming at long-term alterations. In contrast to that, playing with the body's various potentials in the context of contemporary dance is bound less to acts of interference that cannot or only slowly be reversed but to a play-

---

85 Cf. Clarke/Cramer/Müller (2011), p. 227.
86 Cf. Clarke/Cramer/Müller (2011), p. 214.
87 Cf. Kleinschmidt (2018), p. 178.
88 Cf. Clarke/Cramer/Müller (2011), p. 215.

ing with various possibilities of constructing and reconstructing the individual own body image.

Working with flexibility and potentiality of bodies in the choreographic context

Ever since an interest in artistic research began to develop in the 1990s, choreography in the context of contemporary dance is often thought as an open, critical, and intervening project that focuses on uncovering and transgressing of conventions.[89] In this context, one can find numerous choreographic works, particularly in the time between the 1990s and the 2010s, that are linked by their common interest in questioning the body's materiality. One of the first examples of this development was the solo "Self Unfinished" (1998) by biologist and choreographer Xavier Le Roy, a piece that marked a turning away from virtuosic body formations as well as from narrative contexts typical in dance theater.[90] As the title already suggests, in "Self Unfinished" Le Roy presents his own body as an unfinished fluid object which, in the course of the performance, passes through diverse, constantly changing stages of body images and thereby defies being clearly readable by the spectator.

In her book "Am Rand der Körper"[91], dance scientist Susanne Foellmer analyzes the works of different contemporary choreographers between 1990 and 2010, among others those by Meg Stuart, William Forsythe, Jeremy Wade, Jerome Bel, Xavier Le Roy, Ester Salomon, and Mette Ingvartsen. In her analysis, Foellmer points out that the different choreographers share a common, central interest in working with bodies that are in the process of evolving.[92] Meg Stuart, for example, researched on confronting bodies with unpredictable situations ranging from loss of control, imbalance, and recovering.[93] Forsythe worked on defocusing, fragmentation, and decentralization of the body within the frame of techniques he developed.[94] Jeremy Wade worked with constant high-speed changes in emotional states, while being interested

---

89 Cf. Kleinschmidt (2018), p. 24ff.
90 Cf. Foellmer, Susanne (2009) Am Rand der Körper. Inventuren des Unabgeschlossenen im Zeitgenössischen Tanz, p. 138.
91 Cf. Foellmer (2009)
92 With regard to bodies in the process of becoming, Foellmer chisels the term of the "grotesque", a term I am not going to follow here, though.
93 Cf. Foellmer (2009), p. 269f.
94 Cf. Foellmer (2009), p. 328.

in undermining familiar representations of the body.[95] And Eszter Salamon experimented with de- and re-shaping the body, while being interested in transforming it into an a-personal object of movement, which is estranged from representations of a human individual.[96]

Even though these choreographers differ in their aesthetics and way of working, they share a common interest in the body as a changeable, fluid, depersonalized phenomenon.[97] By applying choreographic strategies of de-composing, fragmenting, mutating, and dis- and re-membering, these choreographers create dance-situations that create process-related, fluctuating, and unstable body images.[98]

Referring to "Self-unfinished", dance scientist André Lepecki writes: "Le Roy proposes an entirely different understanding of what a body is: not a stable, fleshy host for a subject, but a dynamic power, an ongoing experiment ready to achieve unforeseeable planes of immanence and consistency."[99] Lepecki's understanding of the body emphasizes a central reference that is used most frequently by artists and theoreticians alike when interested in the notion of a changeable, fluid body.

This reference is the concept of the body without organs, proposed by Gilles Deleuze and Félix Guattari.[100] The body without organs is part of a philosophy in which Deleuze and Guattari turn away from thinking in fixed categories and binaries. In their concept of the body without organs, the body is thought of as "insignificant" as well as in a process of constant disintegration.[101] Therefore, according to Deleuze and Guattari, the body without organs turns into a dynamic becoming which consists of manifold layers and intensities, that crosslink rhizomatically and are basically infinite.[102]

The perspectives of dance scientists Foellmer and Lepecki hint at the fact that many contemporary choreographers, particularly in the 1990s and at the

---

95 Cf. Foellmer (2009), p. 245.
96 Cf. Foellmer (2009), p. 35.
97 Cf. Foellmer (2009), p. 154.
98 Cf. Foellmer (2009), p. 129.
99 Cf. Lepecki, André (2006) Exhausting Dance. Performance and the politics of mouvement, p. 41ff.
100 Cf. Deleuze, Gilles; Guattari, Felix (1987) A Thousand Plateaus, p. 149–166 and p. 232–309.
101 Cf. Deleuze/Guattari (1987), p. 161ff.
102 Cf. Deleuze/Guattari (1987), p. 249, p. 13ff. and also p. 215.

beginning of the 2000s, shared an interest in looking upon the body as a transitory passage, a body that could potentially be anything and that therefore should not be expected to offer a particular meaning.[103] Or to say it with the words of choreographer Jérome Bel:

> "It is at exactly this moment, as I am writing, that I would be able to enumerate all my bodies: Gilles Deleuze, Marie Zorn, Marc Deputter, Antoine Lengo, Madame Bovary [...] Xavier Le Roy, Frédéric Seguette and Lila (his cat), Ballett Frankfurt, Suzanne Lafont, (I am aware that her bodies are Jean-François Lyotard, Samuel Beckett and Vilma, her adopted daughter), Myriam Van Imschoot [...] Hegel (unfortunately), [...], Myriam Gourfink (she has just called), David Cronenberg, [...] Claude Ramey (an invention, yet who might actually exist), [...] Peggy Phelan, [...], Tom Cruise, [...]"[104]

While in the 1990s and the 2000s, the interest in working with a flexible body was often linked to an interest in denying identification through constant disruptions in the readability of bodies, in many more recent choreographic works I observe a shift of focus with regard to the body as an "ongoing experiment".[105] Following the recent works of choreographers such as Antonia Baehr, Mette Ingvartsen, Marie Topp, or Ursina Tossi, I observe that the flexibility and openness of bodies is used as a starting point for developing alternative body images with regard to a specific social topic or question.

In her work "The artificial nature project" (2012), for example, choreographer Mette Ingvartsen is interested in the relationship between the animate and the inanimate world. Her specific aim of creating a choreography in which human movement is not at the center of attention any more, results in a choreographic concept in which the only function of the human performers' bodies is to serve different material on stage, such as a huge amount of confetti

---

103 This interest was also connected with a critical examination of the concept of authorship. In this context, it was also about rejecting clearly recognizable choreographic styles, not becoming a recognizable label that could be easily "marketed" by organizers.
104 Foellmer (2009), p. 22.
105 As the contemporary dance field is highly diverse, I do not refer to the contemporary dance field in general. Neither is this assumption based on empiric research but it is based on my individual perception as a contemporary choreographer working in the field and following the artistic works of other choreographers, such as Antonia Baehr, Meg Stuart, Mette Ingvartsen, Lea Moro, Sheena McGrandels, Ursina Tossi, Reut Shemesh, Marie Topp, Ian Kaler, to name a few.

particles and golden shimmering plastic sheets . Here, Ingvartsen reduces the movement of the human bodies to throw those materials into the air, with the help of their hands and other objects. Supported by light and sound, different landscapes and scenarios from abstract sculpture, glittering fireworks, to apocalyptic environmental disaster emerge.

Based on my assumption that, in more recent choreographic works, the flexibility and openness of bodies is used as a starting point for developing alternative body images with regard to a specific social topic or question, one could state that, at least from the spectators' perspective, Ingvartsen uses the openness of bodies in "The artificial nature project" to explore and propose alternative relationships between human and non-human bodies on stage. By staging bodies whose physical movements of heaving, shooting, throwing, scattering, trickling, rummaging, and digging exclusively serve the functional goal of initiating movement in the surrounding materials, Ingvartsen stages a mutual dependence between human and non-human bodies, which produces a temporal equality between them. Dressed in identical functional clothing, hoods, protective masks, and safety glasses, the different performers' bodies can hardly be identified as individuals.

Although "The artificial nature project" could probably also be perceived as a purely abstract, aesthetic performance, in my opinion, the particular body images that Ingvartsen created can also be read as an artistic proposal that ties in with acute environmental debates, critically dealing with the human's place in his*her environment. By staging human bodies that serve non-human forms of being, Ingvartsen uses the artistic field to create possible imaginations concerning an alternative relationship to nature.

A different approach to the body's potentials can be found in the work "Abecedarium Bestiarium" (2013) by choreographer and performer Antonia Baehr. For "Abecedarium Bestiarium", Baehr invited various artist friends to develop a composition on an extinct animal species of their own choice. In this concept, each animal was linked to a letter, e.g. S like the peaceful Steller manatee that never returned an attack, or T like the Tasmanian tiger that refused to procreate within the confines of a zoo. Baehr expected the compositions to reflect on the relationship between her and her respective friends as well as the affinity between human being and animal.

In her performance of the different compositions, Baehr plays with the transgression of her human body image. By employing performative means such as, for example, extreme changes in her voice, movements and facial expressions, and by combining those changes with costumes and masks, Baehr plays with the affinities between her own body and those of animals. That way, various hybrid creatures made up of human and animal – some of them funny, others frightening, disturbing, or delicate –are produced. In my perception as a spectator, Baehr's human body disappears more and more during the course of the presentation.

At the same time that I, as a spectator, witness how Baehr stages the affinities between her own and the different animal bodies, I experience how familiar physical categories such as male, female, human, or animal become obscure. Therefore, the particular body images Baehr creates and performs also confront the spectators with their own potential proximity to the extinct animals performed on stage. Thus, Baehr's work creates in me as a spectator a strange form of empathy with the other species which is, at the same time, accompanied by a certain feeling of melancholy. After all, it is the human animal that is responsible for the extinction of the Dodo, the Tasmanian Tiger, the Steller Manatee, and many others.

Another artistic approach in using the potentials of the body to experiment with the creation of particular body images can be found in Tümay Kılınçel's choreographic work 'Dansöz' (2019). In 'Dansöz', Kılınçel investigates the question why in the field of contemporary dance, which comprises a huge variety of expressions as well as openness, certain forms of dancing, such as belly dancing, are actually excluded.[106] In an extensive research, Kılınçel examines both practical belly dancing techniques as well as the exoticized and eroticized body image of the female dancers in belly dancing. An interesting aspect of Kılınçel's exploration is her particular cultural relationship to belly dance. Educated as a contemporary dancer, belly-dancing as a physical practice is unknown to her. However, at the same time, Kılınçel feels a connection to this dance form, since it is linked to the cultural roots of her Turkish-born family. In the context of her artistic work, Kılınçel searches for her individual approach by appropriating various movements, clichés, and body images from belly dancing with the help of performative means. In 'Dansöz', Kılınçel performs her subjective understanding of this dance form while simultaneously situating it in the context of contemporary dance field.

---

106 Cf. Tümay Kilincel- Artist talk: https://soundcloud.com/hau-hebbel-am-ufer/tumay-kilincel-artisttalk (date accessed 8 January 2021)

In an interview[107], Kılınçel talks about her initial fear of dealing with the topic within the contemporary dance field. The choreographer describes her fear of stereotypical labels and discrimination, which made her call her work on "Dansöz" a "process of detoxing the own fears as well as the belly-dance body images". Reflecting on Kılınçel's statement, one could assume that, in this case, the concept of the body as a medium and place for self-formation also offers emancipatory potential. By generating alternative body images of belly dancing and performing them as an integral part of "Dansöz", Kılınçel turns her work into a self-determined construction of an identity – for herself and for the spectator.

As much as the works outlined above differ in topic and aesthetics, in my opinion, they also share a feature. This common feature lies in the particular artistic interest of using the performer's body as a place and medium for researching alternative body images through performative means. In this context, the three works could also be understood as artistic imaginations on temporal performative concepts of the self.

In contrast to the neoliberal social context, in which working on and with the body is meant to serve mainly one's own self-control and self-optimization, the artistic works outlined above offer far more freedom of action. This freedom of action is used to develop alternative ideas and imaginations regarding the body, which can also be connected to social questions and topics, such as the relationship between humans and nature, the relationship between humans and animals, or the debate on discrimination against minorities. Much as the works are diverse, they share, in my view, the common factor that they use choreography as a tool to imagine, rehearse, and perform potentially different, temporary body- and self-images that will irritate, expand, or rewrite existing social norms and categories concerning the body.

However, in his book "Vermögende Körper",[108] dance scientist Stefan Hölscher raises the issue that also in the field of choreography, bodies are confronted with external power structures. In reference to Foucault's concept of biopolitics[109], Hölscher states that biopolitical bodies are captured with

---

107 Cf. Tümay Kilincel- Artist talk: https://soundcloud.com/hau-hebbel-am-ufer/tumay-kilincel-artisttalk (date accessed 8 January 2021)
108 Apostolou- Hölscher (2015) Vermögende Körper. Zeitgenössischer Tanz zwischen Ästhetik und Biopolitik.
109 Also cf. p. 36f. of this paper

regard to technique and style, and are functionalized in their expressions.[110] As a counter concept to the biopolitical body, Hölscher suggests the concept of a "vermögender Körper" (capable body), which he places inside the aesthetic context of choreography.[111] Hölscher defines this capable body as a potential and uncertain body that, unlike the biopolitical body, is not exploited for functional purposes. Yet, Hölscher claims that this body is not present automatically even in the aesthetic context of contemporary choreography, since even here, Hölscher suspects a danger of biopolitical capture.

Hölscher locates this danger in the particular way that choreographers work with the body in their respective working processes. In reference to dance scientist Randy Martin, Hölscher looks critically on the widely used practice of improvisation, which he describes as a biopolitical mode of production par excellence. Hölscher criticizes that, in this particular practice, the dancers are supposed to make use of the abilities of their own living bodies, but at the same time, they are expected to produce only raw material, which is then picked from and appropriated by a choreographer who re-contextualizes these materials.[112]

Hölscher criticizes those "biopolitical" choreographic approaches that subject physical movements to pre-set rules and procedures.[113] It is precisely because the capable body, in an aesthetic context, is considered to be a potential body, that, according to Hölscher, one cannot prescribe a fixed technique that would adequately represent it. Therefore, Hölscher insists that the choreographer's task is to examine alternatives to what is already functionalized through techniques.[114]

In reference to performance theorist and dramaturge Bojana Cvejić, Hölscher considers choreography to be a procedure of creating relationships[115], a procedure which does not use fixed forms and techniques, but puts the body in relation to specific materials and ideas, thus facilitating constant processes of physical transformation. The aim of this particular choreographic

---

110 Cf. Apostolou – Hölscher (2015), p. 219.
111 Cf. Apostolou – Hölscher (2015), p. 28.
112 Cf. Apostolou – Hölscher (2015), p. 293.
113 Cf. Apostolou – Hölscher (2015), p. 32.
114 Cf. Apostolou – Hölscher (2015), p. 23.
115 Cf. Cvejic, Bojana (2009) Schnittverfahren und Mischungen. In: tanz-journal, May 2009, p. 29ff.

approach, as Hölscher states, is to constantly keep open the question of what a body can actually be.[116]

Theoretically comprehensible as it may be in relation to Deleuze and Guattari, Hölscher's thesis that, in contemporary choreography, "beliebige" (arbitrary) bodies, arbitrary movements and arbitrary procedures are presented on stage[117] poses a problem from a practical production point of view: Even if bodies are thought of as open in the contemporary choreographic context, to which I undoubtedly agree, in my view, choreographic practice can hardly stay uncertain. Thus, the body's ability to be any variety of things is linked to a concrete physical process of setting the body in motion. The starting point for this process, however, is a specific choreographic framing (such as an interest, task, question, or object) with which the body can actively deal. From the practical perspective of a choreographer, this framing, this outside, however, can hardly remain uncertain or undefined in artistic practice.

Unlike Hölscher, who argues, from the perspective of reception theory, that capable bodies are indeterminate bodies that dwell in the realm of hesitation and procrastination, in the present work I examine how working with an open and potential body might work on the concrete level of choreographic practice.

---

116 Cf. Apostolou – Hölscher (2015), p. 33.
117 Cf. Apostolou – Hölscher (2015), p. 35.

3. On Methods
The gap between what we are & what we are not

The initial question of this research – how can the openness and negotiability of the body be used for purposes other than self-optimization – led to an exploration of the body as a place and medium in which the individual can experience a process of becoming unfamiliar or even alien to the own self. In the context of this work, I consider the body as twofold, i.e., as a subject that is the place of individual experience and perception and as an object that can be used intentionally and reflected on. Based on this particular understanding of the body, I consider the "self" as the unity of the body subject and the body object.[1]

In my particular research on performative strategies that can be used to become unfamiliar to the own self, Gallagher's concept of the body image was a central reference point. According to Gallagher, the body image includes three things:[2] Firstly, it includes the body as it is perceived in the immediate consciousness. Secondly, it includes the conceptual construct of the body. And thirdly, it includes the emotional attitude and feelings about the body. In Gallagher's view, all three aspects are open to change and, therefore, the body image is open to change, too. In the context of my research, based on Gallagher's concept of the body image, I assumed that my interest in using the body to become unfamiliar to the own self could be practically approached by exploring ways of consciously creating unfamiliar body images.

According to the specific profile of the graduate program "Performing Citizenship" as an artistic and scientific hybrid, my research process took place on two levels. On a theoretical level, I researched on different theoretical perspectives on the body, focusing on the question how body images are individually and socially constructed. My approach to these theoretical perspectives was

---

1 Cf. Gugutzer (2002), p. 67.
2 Cf. Gallagher (1986), p. 545f.

characterized by the following question: What kind of choreographic strategies could be derived from those theoretical perspectives when researching on a non-optimizing and non-controlling approach to the body.

The practical artistic research can be described as a process of practical experiments on how body images can be actively recreated with the help of performative tools. For the practical research I invited a group of several co-researchers.[3] Those co-researchers took part in the practical experiments and shared their practical experiences as well as interests in the reflections on the experiments. In my particular role as artistic research director, I had different functions. Based on the research topic, I developed several practical experiments that I introduced to the co-researchers. Those experiments implied two perspectives, an internal perspective of conducting the experiment and an external perspective of witnessing the experiment. After each experiment, the different individual experiences (from the internal and external perspective) were verbally shared and also documented.

As artistic research director, I collected and documented the different experiences of both perspectives, by making notes as well as by sound- and video recordings. Throughout the experiments, all co-researchers, including myself, changed perspective between conducting and witnessing the experiments.[4] In the following, whenever I refer to the group of co-researchers including myself as the artistic research director, I use the term research group.

On a practical level, one method that I used in both practical research projects can be described as consciously creating gaps between what the body is and what the body is not yet. In the first research project "the bodies we are", I created this gap by confronting the co-researchers' bodies with photos of bodies with which they did not identify. In the second research project, "Let's face it!", I created this gap by working with the unfamiliar or even fictitious body images of a body with no face, a body with plenty of faces, and a face without a body.

Another working method that I used in both artistic research projects to actively deal with those gaps can be described as a choreographic strategy of appropriation. In the context of this work, I consider appropriation as an artistic

---

[3] The co-researchers of the first research project were: Sophie Aigner, Juli Reinartz, Vania Rovisco and Johanna Roggan. The co-researchers of the second research project were: Sophie Aigner and Vania Rovisco.

[4] Although I took part in the practical physical exploration, in comparison to the co-researchers, I spent more time in the role of outsider spectator.

strategy that includes the borrowing of a pre-existing image, object, or idea. I assume that, by appropriating details or features of other bodies in the form of a particular perception, gesture, movement, body description etc., individuals can potentially affect the individual body and self-perception. On a theoretical level, this understanding of appropriation is similar to Waldenfels, who describes appropriation as "a way of recognition and an attempt to contextualize the undefined, the yet unknown or disturbing"[5] In the context of my research, this process of appropriation implied several steps, which I will shorty outline in the following.

Collecting

In the beginning of each artistic research project, as artistic research director, I set particular frames that were connected to the research topic. For the first research project "The bodies we are", this frame was the task "Collect photos or images of bodies that you do not identify with". For the second research project "Let's face it!", this frame was the decision to research on particular unfamiliar and even fictitious body images, namely on a body without a face, a face without a body, and a body with plenty of faces. Accordingly, both artistic research projects started from the subjective perceptions of the individuals taking part in the research.

Despite this subjective research approach, the individual thoughts, feelings, and associations on the bodies collected cannot be completely separated from actual social discourses on the body.[6] Assuming that how individuals subjectively perceive and think bodies is at least partly influenced by the norms and values of the social context in which they are situated,[7] the selected photos and images of bodies also gave hints to social inclusions and exclusions of bodies within our present society. I am aware that this method of collecting images of bodies that one does not identify with might raise critical remarks, since the fact that those bodies were labeled as unfamiliar bodies simultaneously marked them as "other" bodies.[8] However, in the particular context of the research, the aim was not to distance ourselves from those bodies, but, quite

---

5   Cf. Waldenfels, Bernhard (1997) Topographie des Fremden, p. 48f.
6   Cf. also p. 36 of this paper.
7   Cf. Gugutzer (2015), p. 8f.
8   It is especially from the perspective of diversity discourses that this labeling as other is problematic, since those discourses aim at including all different bodies, and try to work against those classifications.

the contrary, to appropriate features of those bodies with the aim of experiencing them in the own body.

Creating an archive of potential body images
After individually collecting the material, I assembled the different photos of bodies the research group did not identify with in the first research project, as well as the various associations concerning bodies without a face, etc., in the second research project. I called this assembly of diverse material "the archive of potential body images".

Individual process of perception & imagination
From this "archive of potential body images", each member of the research group intuitively chose one photo which, in the following, became the working base for examining the individual perception of this body. The focus of those perception-experiments was the following question: What do the individuals of the research group see, think, associate, and imagine when looking at, and perceiving, each of those chosen bodies? Based on Merleau-Ponty's understanding of perception as a selective process, which can never perceive the totality of an object, but picks out and focuses on particular details[9], I considered the perception of the selected bodies on photos as an individual and selective process. I combined this subjective process of perceiving the unfamiliar body images with a method of simultaneously describing the individual perception in written form.

Documenting the individual perception
The method I used to document and collect the research group's individual perceptions was based on the surrealist technique of "automatic writing"[10]. Assuming that the particular way in which individuals perceive bodies is also subconsciously affected by particular social norms concerning the body, including its inclusions and exclusions, its stereotypes, etc.[11], I was looking for a method that allowed us not only to reproduce those stereotypes, but to develop a preferably wider range of imaginations and associations related to the photos selected.

---

9   Cf. Merleau-Ponty (2012), p 69ff.
10 Cf. for example: Conner, Janet (2009) Writing down your soul: How to activate and listen to the extraordinary voice within
11 Also cf. p. 36f. of this paper.

In many artistic and also psychological contexts, the practice of "automatic writing" is employed for collecting spontaneous associations with a topic or object of interest. The idea behind it is that a continuous and, most importantly, fast writing process will allow the free flow of one's individual associations and prevent it from being judged and self-censored first.

In my own research process, I applied this method of automatic writing to facilitate a form of individual perception that is open to any potential description of bodies, even if the descriptions and imaginations that came up during this free flow of associations appeared to be strange, weird, or unusual. I assumed that, with the help of this method, the individual imaginations would bring up unusual ideas and associations which could potentially create new perspectives on the bodies selected.

In this method of "automatic writing", the individual perceptions of the research members were translated into language. Hence, the method of "automatic writing" enabled a change from individual subjective perception to a verbalization of this perception, thus becoming shareable with others. By writing down what each individual of the research group saw, felt, and imagined when looking at these images, a broad variety of descriptions was created. Those descriptions included body parts, names, categories, potential activities, fantasies, and desires for each of the selected body images.

Building scores

The collection of all written descriptions became the source from which to build performative scores. I then asked all members of the research group to create performative scores[12] by intuitively picking four to six words or short sentences and putting them together on a short list. Thus, in the research process, a "performative score" was the combination of the initially described body images and the short list of intuitively assembled related descriptions. Those scores were the starting point for a practical movement research.

Moving the scores

In this step, the performers started a movement exploration in which they practically moved into the descriptions and images by appropriating them on

---

12 In the performative art field there are many understandings of the concept of a "score". For more information about the concept of score in contemporary performing arts, also cf: Burrows, Jonathan (2010) Scores, studios, improvisation, p. 141–151. In: A choreographer's handbook

an individual physical level. While in the method of automatic writing, the individual perception was translated into language-based descriptions, in this step, descriptions and image were translated into movement.

During the exploration of the score we additionally worked with the method of inner focus. This method assumes that, by focusing on a particular body part, a way of breathing, a relation between different parts of the body, etc., one can create specific inner perceptions of the own body, which then generates correlating movements, gestures and perceptions in the performers' bodies. Since the performers physically performed those movements and perceptions, the appropriated image and its descriptions could be observed from the outside. This performative translation through movement exceeded the static image by setting the static image and its descriptions in motion. What I considered central in this process was the change of perspective. Whereas in the steps before, the described bodies were perceived as "other" bodies, perceived as separate from the own self, in this step, the process of physically appropriating features of those bodies blurred the separation between the own self and the other. In this process, the own individual body became the place and medium in which alternative body images could be perceived and performed.

Before starting the physical exploration of the scores, I shared with the co-researchers a map of several questions. These questions were offered as choreographic parameters for translating the static images and their verbal descriptions into performative movement material:

Are there body parts that are central for the particular body?
(Head, torso, arms, hands, legs, face, mouth, anus, organs, etc.)
Are there particular movements or a particular movement quality
in this body part?

Which actions do you associate with this body?

Is there a special relation to time?
(quick, slow, active, inactive, etc.)

Is there a particular emotional state
that you associate with this body?

Which organs of perception are central?
(mouth, nose, eyes, ears, skin)

> What is the anatomical structure of this body?
> Is there any detail that strikes you?

How is the breath?
(short, long, calm, agitated, resilient, flat, deep)
Where does the breath go?
(stomach, breast, mouth)

> How is the body tension?
> (relaxed, tense, or different tensions in different body parts?)

How does the body relate to space?
(oriented to the outside space, oriented to the inside,
closeness, distance, etc.)

> Are there particular desires or imaginations
> that you connect with that body?

Given these questions, the different members of the research group started to physically translate the scores and the related photos of other bodies into particular movements, gestures, postures, body tensions, emotional states, relations to space, etc. This process of physically performing this material in turn affected the own self-perception of the performers. In the context of my research, I considered this process of physically appropriating characteristics of a seemingly unfamiliar body as a potential strategy of playfully reconstructing the own internal body image.

As a conclusion, my research method could be described as a continuous translation between different levels – from the level of subjective perception to the level of verbalizing the individual perception and making it sharable, to the level of physically appropriating those descriptions, the latter again producing particular subjective experiences (in the person moving as well as in the spectator witnessing the experiment from outside). These processes of translation are bound to create gaps, since with every translation, a jump happens, which adds new information and experiences. My research method could be described as a mutual inspiration between theory and practice. Theoretical perspectives influenced the artistic research process, and vice versa, the insights generated in the artistic research influenced the scientific reading.

4. The first artistic research project "The bodies we are"

In the first artistic research project "The bodies we are", I focused on the following questions: How does the process of creating body images within the choreographic process actually work? Where are the limits to this process? And: How can the process of consciously recreating body images be used as a chance to become unfamiliar to the own self?

Thus, throughout the first artistic research project, I tried to tackle the negotiability of body images from a particular perspective, i.e. that of temporarily becoming the other, of becoming unfamiliar to the own self.[1] My proposal of "becoming unfamiliar to the own self" is meant to be understood as a potential counter-concept to the present social imposition of optimization and control of the body, a concept which aims at self-improvement and self-control, yet by precisely this logic urgently needs to avoid and suppress the different, the unexpected or the unknown. In this context of my research, I considered becoming the other, becoming unfamiliar, as a strategy to expand the known range of the individual body- and self-perceptions.

To do research on the questions above, for the first part of my artistic research project, I invited four different female collaborators: Sophie Aigner (visual artist), Juli Reinartz (choreographer, performer), Johanna Roggan (choreographer, dancer) and Vania Rovisco (choreographer, performer). We worked together in residence for three weeks, from February 9 to 29, 2016, at PACT Zollverein in Essen, Germany.

---

1   In the context of this work, I consider the self as the entity of the body subject (the body as a perceiving and sensing subject) and the body object (the intentional use of the body, the verbal reflection). Cf. Gugutzer (2002), p. 67. Since both how the body perceives itself and how the body is used and reflected on are open to change, the self is not a stable entity.

4.1 Preparing the research. A collection of bodies we are not

A few days prior to our residency at PACT Zollverein, I sent an email to each of the four co-researchers involved in the planned research, asking them to bring pictures or photographs of human bodies that fascinated them, but that they could not identify with or felt a notable emotional distance to. On the first day of our research, we simply looked at the diverse visual material contributed, that of bodies covered in body-oil, of punks, of wrestlers, of body-builders, of obese bodies, of Siamese twins, of bodies without a face, of transgender bodies, cyborgs, bodies with artificial limbs, anorexic bodies, the body of Rebecca Horn in her mask made of pencils, and several others.

We sat together in one of the studios of PACT Zollverein, surrounded by a collection of diverse images of bodies that, on a subjective level, seemingly did not represent us. What was striking, when looking at them, was that many of the collected bodies had one or several "extreme" features in their appearance. There were, for example, "extremely" massive or "extremely" muscular bodies, bodies with a very exalted way of dressing, bodies with an unusual anatomical structure, etc. Reflecting on this subjective selection, one could state that, within our research group, what was perceived as unfamiliar were bodies that differed in one or the other way from the neoliberal body ideal of the trained, healthy, and controlled body.

The fact that the bodies collected by us were not physically present in the room, not in person, but only as visual material, at the same time determined the way we could approach them. This basic situation offered us the freedom to acknowledge and to allow our feeling of distance from those depicted bodies without having to worry about hurting anyone personally. What exactly was it, then, that we perceived in those bodies and that had led to our feeling of distance from them? To be able to arrive at an answer to this question, we applied a method that combines the observing of the visual material and the set skill of 'automatic writing'[2].

Experiment:

Take ten minutes to look at the depicted body below and, while doing so, write down everything and anything that spontaneously comes to your mind about this body. Within those ten minutes, do not stop writing.

---

2   Cf. also chapter – 3: On Methods, p. 58f.

4. The first artistic research project "The bodies we are"

Image: Loloi, Yossi (2010) The full beauty project. Cf. http://www.yossil oloi.com/portfolio/fullbeauty-project/ (date accessed 9 February 2022)

Text extracts:

Reinartz: She sits there in her full fleshy splendor and I somehow want to reach inside her. Or I would like to be her, I would like to have this mass around me, to reach inside me, to carry weight, to sweat, to feel my flesh on my flesh. I would like to grab hold of myself, to haul myself along, to allow myself to fall, to drape myself around me, to treat my own body the way I treat the body of others, to organize my dead mass, to touch it, to sense it, to carry it. I always want to know where I am, to be able to see myself at any moment, and to locate myself. Then I want to shake my mass, move it, feel its heaviness, its weight, and I want to perceive my cells and immigrate into them.

Velsinger: There is gravity at work, the movements need more open space, the body consists of padding filled with air and fat, it keeps dripping, a monstrous body, oval forms, the waviness of the flesh, lust, mass and volume unite and become something alien, it is abound, it is exorbitant, unlimited excess, monster, being pushed, being helpless, acts of sensuousness, skin folds, more and more wrinkles and folds, simultaneity of flesh and flesh and fat and liquid, the body consists of lots of different breasts that feed others, but want to be fed themselves at the same time, time to spare.

Although both individual texts evolved as the result of a subjective observation and both writers emphasized their own different aspects, one can still detect significant similarities. In the selected examples, the different written reactions to and associations with the body overlapped with regard to the description of physical characteristics such as significant weight, bodily massiveness, and volume. The experiment also made it clear that describing physical characteristics such as, in this case, massiveness and volume simultaneously triggered additional internal images or associations concerning that particular physicality. Even if those internal images were expressed in different words, a similarity in fascination with that body can be noticed. One might call this an ambivalent fascination with a huge or massive body, lustfully extending into the surrounding space. In a way, the collected descriptions on this body could also be read as a radical counter-concept to that of the disciplined and controlled body of the achievement-oriented neoliberal society. A body that lustfully expands to overflow, a body that simply does not seem to stop expanding in order to feed itself and also others and to create lust.

In the next step of the artistic research process, the research group examined the physical appropriation of the descriptions and imaginations, with the particular interest in creating unfamiliar internal body- and self-perceptions. Before I continue to reflect on this practical research, I will briefly enter the field of theory, referring to Merleau-Ponty to explain the particular role of movement and perception in the process of creating and recreating internal body images.

4.2 Theoretical perspective: How the body image can be influenced by action and perception

According to the phenomenologist Merleau-Ponty, what is unique about the body is that it has an internal dimension as well as an external dimension. That is why the body has the capacity of double sensations, allowing it to alternate between the two functions of "touching" and "being touched".³ Consequently, the body exists in two ways – as an object that is "being touched", which is a visual body that consists of flesh, bones, organs, etc., and as a subject that is a "touching" body, or the carrier of the senses, that consists of sensory perception.

Although these two bodies coexist, their two functions are different. While the body defined as an intersection of bones, muscles, and flesh is an object that can be used and possessed, the lived body[4] (i.e. the body as subject) is actively engaged in dealing with the world through perceptual experience. Through actively moving in space and using its senses, the body as subject perceives the world through seeing, smelling, hearing, tasting, and sensing it. This is why Merleau-Ponty characterizes the body not only as an object but also as a subject or an agent, which he defines as our medium to receive and transmit our surrounding environment[5].

Since perception is linked to one single perspective, Merleau-Ponty states that, when perceiving an object, an individual does not perceive the object as a whole. Instead, individual perception is a selective process which does not cover all details of the perceived object.[6] Since what is perceived is subjective and also depends on what raises individual interests, thoughts, and desires,[7] the process of perception can be considered as a selective process that creates the perceived object or environment. Therefore, when researching on strategies of actively creating body images, the body as subject or agent is of central importance: Because of its capacity of double sensations, the body is not only the medium to perceive and build the outside environment through this perception, but simultaneously is also the medium to perceive and therefore build the own self through perception.

This process is complex. Merleau-Ponty points out that the body perceiving its own self is a synthesis of visual, tactile, and motor aspects, while those three aspects of the body are interconnected through permanent communication.[8] Thus, the process of self-perception can be initiated through a particular

---

3 Cf. Merleau-Ponty (2012), p. 95.
4 In the original French version, Merleau-Ponty used the term "le corps propre". In German, the lived body is often translated as Leib. In the context of this work, whenever I refer to the body as a perceiving body, I use the expression body as subject.
5 Cf. Merleau-Ponty (2012), p. 69ff.
6 Cf. Merleau-Ponty (2012), p. 72f.
7 Cf. Merleau-Ponty (2012), p. 84.
8 Cf. Merleau-Ponty (2012), p. 150.

movement, through a particular sensation or touch, as well as through visualization. The interconnectedness of those three aspects leads to the fact that a particular movement or touch is able to produce a particular visualization of the body. For example, when one clenches the foot inside the shoe, one can instantly "visualize" the foot, although it is hidden. But it also functions the other way round: the visualization of a particular body part in most cases calls forth a particular sensation or movement.

Merleau-Ponty points out that, due to the synthesis of the body's visual, tactile, and motor aspects, humans are also able to see themselves through an inner eye as well as to visualize parts of the body that they have never seen, but experienced through tactile or motor aspects. What is characteristic within this process of self-perception is that the conscious perception of the own body never includes all aspects of the body simultaneously. The contrary is the case: the perception of the own body necessarily leads to a focus on one or a limited amount of particular parts, such as the foot, the organs, the skin, the weight, etc. By focusing on specific aspects and simultaneously displacing the perception of other potential aspects of the body, a specific self-perception is created that would change if the focus lay on other parts of the body.

Coming back to the question of how one can actively use the openness of the body for other aims than optimization and control, the phenomenological concept of the body as agent is helpful. Since the perception of the own self is linked to the interconnectedness of the body's visual, tactile and motor aspects, the perception of the own body can be influenced very much depending on how the body is moved and used, what kinds of sensations are produced and how the body is visualized. And although all of those aspects are strongly influenced and also determined by the particular social context a body is situated in[9], in principle, they also leave space for individual negotiation. In other words: Although in daily life we are guided by socially determined movement and sensation patterns which imply numerous physical practices of shaping, training, purifying, correcting, controlling, or rejuvenating bodies, etc., in theory, there is a potential at any moment for developing alternative ways of using and perceiving the body.

---

9   Cf. Crossley, Nick (2001) The social body. Habit, identity and desire, p. 5.

4.3 Artistic experiments: Appropriating unfamiliar actions and perceptions

In the practical artistic research process, perceiving and describing other bodies that appeared to be unfamiliar to us functioned as a first step to find out what each individual of the research group actually saw in those collected bodies. In a second step of the practical research, I considered each of those bodies collected to be a potential space for alternative actions and perceptions. By collecting the descriptive texts of all the team members I separated the subjective descriptions from the individual co-researchers and rearranged the descriptions into a heterogeneous archive of observations, which were then used as a pool of resource material to generate performative scores from.[10]

Example for a score:
Your name is Full Beauty // digging into of one's own masses of flesh // expanding // becoming exorbitant // skin-folds // being of enormous volume and weight and wanting to expose it // straining time
(time frame: 20 minutes)

In the scores, we put together particular actions and perceptions that had been derived from the collected descriptions. Dealing with those scores, the performers[11] were asked to appropriate the particular body descriptions and associations and individually translate them into movement as well as body perceptions. In the very beginning, this created a rather obvious problem: How could the performers move and perceive their own body as massive, if their own physical appearance was not massive at all? What kind of performative strategies could bridge those gaps in mass, volume, and weight? Or was the experiment and, thus, also the possibility of consciously recreating the internal body image getting to its limits?

---

10   In the context of this research, I understood the writing of 'scores' not as a representation of the following performance, but as a practical tool for generating and providing information for improvised performative actions, without prescribing their final realization.

11   In my following reflections on the practical artistic experiments, when I refer to a co-researcher or me doing and/or watching a practical experiment, I use the terms performer and spectator or observer.

In order to tackle this challenge of the difference between imagination and fact, we applied the method of inner focusing. Here, we focused our attention strictly to the bodies weight, its mass and volume.[12] In this physical exploration of the body's weight, mass and volume, lots of questions arose which the performers then used for their individual physical explorations, such as: What exactly is it in a body that has mass and weight, what actually is it that potentially expands in a body, and how does it expand? What material does the body's mass consist of – flesh, fat, bones, organs, etc.? What influence do weight and volume have on breathing? What is the relationship between mass and weight on the one hand, and gravity on the other?

As a result of our inner shift of perceptional focus on the weight and volume of the body, we experimented with various types of action laid down in the scores, such as, for example, "wanting to expose the volume to view", "draping the mass around oneself", "dancing in a club", "lifting an arm", "jumping into the water", and so on. In this process of appropriating details of the described photos of other, seemingly unfamiliar bodies, the performers discovered features and details in and with their own bodies, which, before, were ascribed to bodies that were subjectively perceived as unfamiliar. In the course of the experiments, an ever more differentiated and actual physical interior process of perception was developed, and, at the same time, a concrete pool of movement material evolved.

In this experimental process of reconstructing the performer's internal body image, it was helpful to use Merleau-Ponty's idea of "synthesis of the body's visual, tactile and motor aspects" for a conscious influencing of the self-perception of one's own body. That way, the inner focus on sensing the body's weight and volume led to a change in self-perception of one's body, from which alternative qualities of movement as well as alternative internal visualizations of the body could be developed. What was interesting in this context, too, was that the inner visualization of one's own body as a massive and expanding body already led to a changed self-perception of that own body.

During the physical experiments, there were several moments when the performers felt frustrated. In those moments, the performers experienced the process of appropriation as a form of pretense, as fake, as mere obeying to prescribed tasks without experiencing any concrete resonance inside their own bodies. From my outside perspective as a spectator or witness of the experiments, I was able to sense those moments, too, and to define them as a result

---

12   For a detailed description of this working method, also cf. p. 60 of this paper.

occurring particularly when the performative score that was too open. In those cases, the process of appropriation remained too much on an intellectual level (i.e. on the level of mental imagination) and could only to a limited degree or even not at all be experienced physically, as well.

Further reasons for the occurrence of problems were those situations in which the respective performer had not (yet), in her own mind, been able to develop an actual interest in appropriating the scope of potential actions and perceptions associated with a massive body. What must certainly be considered in this context is that massive and heavy bodies are clearly stigmatized by our Western neoliberal society, a fact which can be assumed to have led to the performers' desire to actually distance themselves from that type of physicality. Yet, this is exactly where a particular interest of the entire artistic experiment becomes relevant, namely the question of what happens when individuals appropriate physical characteristics that, for personal reasons or those influenced by social norms, they cannot, do not want to, or even are not supposed to identify with?

Here, our artistic research touched issues and questions that are also broached by the body positivity movement.[13] I am aware that the particular approach of our artistic research project to identify, for example, massive bodies as unfamiliar could also be perceived as problematic in the perspective of the body positivity movement. By categorizing those bodies as "other" or "unfamiliar", the research project could be accused of reproducing a social discrimination against non-normalized bodies. In my opinion, however, this critique would leave one central aspect of the research project unconsidered. In the particular context of this research, considering bodies as unfamiliar at no point aimed at discriminating or excluding any form of body. The contrary is the case – by physically appropriating details of seemingly unfamiliar bodies and appropriating some of their features, the research project aimed at blurring the separation between the own and the other and enlarging the potentials of what the own body could actually be and become.

---

13 The body positivity movement is a social movement initially created to empower overweight individuals, to criticize unrealistic and discriminating body ideals, and to fight for more diversity. The movement, which is especially present in social media, claims the acceptance of all bodies, regardless of physical ability, gender, race, size, or appearance. Cf. for example: Raikwar, Nikita (2016) Body Positivity. Tackling Negative Body Image. Or: Michelberger, Melodie (2021) Body Politics.

In this regard, the process of appropriation could be understood as a challenge of temporarily adopting something unfamiliar or other than one's own. By doing that, the performers received access to physical and sensuous experiences they could not anticipate before. The unfamiliar self-perceptions that were created during this process not only affected the movements and perceptions of the performers, but they also lead to the temporal development of alternative interests as well as alternative desires and pleasures regarding the own body.

Our research process can therefore be looked upon as an experimental field with regard to the question of what variety of alternative actual proprioceptions are generated through the process of appropriation, and what alternative interests, desires, or forms of lust can be experienced or made possible in this way. In this context, it was Juli Reinartz's process of appropriation that was particularly interesting. In her initial imaginations and associations that she expressed in the description of the body of "Full Beauty", Reinartz did not at any point link that body with the concept of a burden or of limitation, but with a deep pleasure at owning so much volume that one can drape one's own body around oneself. One could say that, in Reinartz's case, that body, which had appeared to be an unfamiliar one at first, developed into a base for projections, both with regard to a desire to grow into more and more mass and to expand excessively into the space, and also with regard to becoming one's own object and subject of lust. The process of appropriation that followed the initial description of the body in the picture transferred this desire into Reinartz's own body.

This desire for extreme voluptuousness with regard to the (female) body is an interesting issue when it comes to societal norms, as it is a minoritized desire in our Western neoliberal society, and radically differs from the logic of optimization and control. Reinartz's fascination with the excessive body, developing while she was appropriating features of that body, therefore also contained a subversive level, as her fascination was equally an objection to the ideal of the slim and disciplined body of today's post-modern capitalism, a body that is arrived at through (constant) self-inflicted physical leisure stress. Simultaneously, and seemingly as a contrast, Reinartz's fascination with an excessive body confronted us with a topic concerning all of us: the topic of the body as a consumer. This consumer body is totally in line with all the expansive dreams of capitalism – a market that expands by creating further needs on its own.

From this ambivalent fascination with the expanding body, alternative images and desires concerning the own body could be developed in the course of the experiments. In order to express and compile these alternative images and desires, all derived from actual physical experience, I set up another experiment. In this experiment, I asked the performer to use language to express all emerging imaginations and associations regarding the own self and body that derived from the particular physical experience.

A sample from Reinartz's text:

"I imagine myself becoming bigger and bigger and softer and softer and more and more. I can see myself, I can feel myself ever-expanding. I can rest on my enormous and soft self, a cascade of folds. Rivulets of sugar crystals pour down my body seeking ever newer valleys and I produce, I generate ever more valleys and ever more mountains. I am becoming heavier and heavier and softer and softer. I can watch myself, watch my own limitless body. We see my breasts, we see my shoulders, we see my knees, we see everything, we see how we turn and when we fall and if we fall, we fall softly, we become softer and softer, we fall more and more softly, we grow forever bigger, we see forever more. And we touch ourselves and grow ever bigger and it (all) doesn't end at all (...)"[14]

At first sight, the imaginations and desires that were articulated by Reinartz in the experiment seem reminiscent of a scene from "Alice in Wonderland" in which the expansion of a body gets out of control. The scripted phantasies on expansion, on growing ever more, on feeling ever more, on noticing ever more, voice a pleasure at exceeding limits that is usually rather ascribed to children. At the same time, Reinartz's text also contained a second level: Based on the new, unfamiliar physical experience, a body full of lust and pleasure is imagined and generated with the help of language that not only actively and endlessly takes in, but also expands endlessly while actually being thrilled by that process. In Reinartz's imagination, this most pleasurable experience can be expanded endlessly, thus increasing exponentially.

Particularly in connection with the present ideal of a disciplined and controlled body – which, in its aim at discipline, simultaneously uses up an unlimited amount of resources – Reinartz's imagined visualization is an interesting counter-concept. For it is a body that translates the limitless into the vast enjoyment of physical sensation and which generates pleasure not through consuming, but through its own physicality, i.e. through itself.

---

14 The text is a transcription of an improvised text Reinartz generated in the context of the experiment.

4. The first artistic research project "The bodies we are"

What the experiment makes clear is that appropriating unfamiliar actions and perceptions that derive from an unfamiliar physicality facilitates a variety of new, unfamiliar desires and phantasies with regard to one's own body. Therefore, the imaginations created during these experiments also form a part of the actual appropriation, yet with language playing a specific role in the process. Relating this articulation through language to Gallagher's definition of the body image[15], in which the body image includes the individual perception of the body, as well as the conceptual construction through language, one could consider the performers' texts as an attempt to use language to create alternative conceptual constructions of their bodies.

In the artistic experiments, language was used as a tool to articulate the individual physical sensations, imagined visualizations, and desires that appeared in the process of appropriation and, thus, to be able to share them with others. It is in this sense that language was used as a kind of voice for potential alternative ideas concerning the body – by which we simultaneously generated alternative discourse on the bodies of the performers. While the body's individual level of perception remains exclusively limited to the interior perspective of the subject involved, the verbal body descriptions and associations allowed for sharing the results with others. To examine further this potential of language as a tool to construct discourse on the body, in the following, I am going to discuss a selection of Judith Butler's theses.

4.4 Theoretical perspective: How the body image can be influenced by labeling and naming

In her theoretical perspective on the body, the philosopher and gender theorist Judith Butler focuses on how actions of naming and labeling the body via the use of language actually constructs the body.[16] Butler considers the body as a "linguistic being"[17] without rejecting the existence of the primary experiences of the body, such as the sensation of flesh or sensory perception. However, she

---

15 Cf. Gallagher (1986), p. 545f.
16 Butler is best known for her gender theory, in which she developed her theory of gender performativity. However, in this chapter, I will not focus on gender issues but I will use her concept of the body as a linguistic being, in order to investigate and show how the body can be thought of as constructed through language and social discourses.
17 Cf. Butler (1997), p. 1f.

does not include them in what she labels the body's materiality. According to Butler, it is not the body's primary physical experiences that constitute its materiality, but the materiality of the body is constituted through language and this language, in turn, represents particular social discourses.[18]

In order to understand Butler's thesis that the body is constructed through language, it is helpful to understand the basic assumptions that precede this claim. Butler's first assumption is that a body is not accessible without the use of language.[19] Based on this thesis, Butler claims that any physical sensation and perception of the own or of another person's body is inevitably linked to language. In other words, according to Butler, when someone perceives the own or a different body, he or she does not perceive a chaotic and unmanageable amount of information, but instead, the action of perceiving a body goes hand in hand with the action of focusing on a particular characteristic, detail, or part of the body. In this process the perceiving individual uses language to give names and labels to what he or she perceives, which Butler understands as an action of creating particular labels and categories.[20]

Based on Foucault's discourse theory[21], Butler understands language not as a neutral system of description, but as something that already carries particular discourses which imply mechanisms of inclusion, exclusion, as well as specific ways of discussing and labeling things and bodies.[22] Butler claims that there is no "pure" or "natural" body[23], because the very moment an individual or an institution refer to a body through the use of language, a particular for-

---

18 Cf. Butler (1993), p. 2.
19 Cf. Butler (1993), p. 11.
20 Cf. Butler (1993), p. 30, also p. 8.
21 According to Foucault, discourse is an instrument of power, as it creates certain categories of thinking which, in turn, control how things are discussed and labeled. This is why Foucault states that in every society, the production of discourse is at once controlled, selected, organized, and redistributed by a certain number of procedures that serve to ward off its powers and dangers, gain mastery over its chance events, and evade its ponderous, formidable materiality. Therefore, according to Foucault, discourse also functions as a system of oppression, since the process of naming and labeling automatically organizes and controls materiality and thereby leads to particular inclusions and exclusions. Cf. Foucault, Michel (1981) The Order of Discourse. In: Robert Young: Untying the text: A Post-Structuralist Reader, p. 52.
22 Cf. Butler (1997), p. 29.
23 Cf. Butler (1993), p. 11.

mation takes place. This process organizes and narrows down a vast and potentially formidable materiality of the body.²⁴

While Foucault's discourse theory expounds that it is impossible for an individual to speak about the body outside of control through discourse, it does not say anything about how language affects the things that are named on a concrete level. In order to argue how and why the process of naming the body in a particular way affects and even constructs the body's materiality, Butler refers to two different speech act theories, borrows the main concepts, and uses them for her own theses.

From the speech act theory of philosopher John L. Austin, Butler borrows the thesis that language is performative and constructs social reality. In his speech act theory, Austin distinguishes "perlocutionary" from "illocutionary" speech acts. A perlocutionary speech act is an utterance that leads to certain effects. For example, someone utters something and, as an effect of this utterance, someone feels scared or insufficient. In a perlocutionary speech act, the utterance is only the base of the speech act and not the same as the act itself. In contrast, an illocutionary speech act does what it says at the very moment of the utterance. To give an example, the judge who says: "I sentence you" is thereby really sentencing someone, or the doctor who says: "It's a girl!" is thereby labeling the newborn and declaring it a girl.

Because of this power to produce concrete effects that, in turn, create a particular reality, Austin considers the illocutionary speech act to be a "performative act".²⁵ Butler connects Austin's thesis that language does what is says with Foucault's concept of discourse. Consequently, being labeled necessarily implies being confronted with certain expectations, norms, values, reactions, etc. Due to this argumentation, Butler develops her particular understanding of performativity:

> "(…) performativity must be understood not as a singular or deliberate 'act', by which a subject brings into being what she/he names, but, rather, as the reiterative and citational practice by which discourse produces the effects that it names."²⁶

---

24   Cf. Butler (1997), p. 5.
25   Cf. Butler (1997), p17.
26   Butler (1993), p. 2.

This understanding of performativity is especially interesting in relation to the current social request for body- and self- optimization. Applying Butler's theory to the neoliberal discourse on controlling and optimizing bodies, one can state that the constant citational practice of labels such as fit, young, controlled, trained, healthy, beautiful, detoxed, etc., implies specific values as well as expectations which, in turn, make individuals behave in a specific way. Therefore, the labels put on bodies through (social) media, science, or other institutions affect the materiality of bodies, since they influence how individuals perceive, use and form their bodies.

While Butler used Austin's theory to show how the process of naming produces effects, she also included the opposite perspective of being named, by borrowing the "concept of interpellation"[27] from Louis Althusser. According to Althusser, it is the interpellation – the process of being named – that forms the subject.[28]

While Althusser limits the notion of interpellation to the action of an individual voice that names a subject, Butler proposes to disconnect interpellation from individual voice and to connect it to the verbal citation of existing convention in social discourse.[29] Consequently, interpellation becomes the instrument and mechanism of discourse that is constantly calling subjects in particular ways.

What is the outcome of combining Austin's concept of the performativity of language with Althusser's concept of interpellation? By doing so, Butler outlines a subject that is constituted in a field defined by two different relations. On the one hand, a subject is constituted through being addressed or being interpellated by another person. On the other hand, through that act from the outside, the subject simultaneously becomes capable of addressing others, and also itself. In other words, the subject is named and constituted by language – and, in turn, the subject itself uses language to allocate names, labels and descriptions to the own as well as to other bodies.

This double relation allows Butler to construct a subject that, though itself constituted by language, is also simultaneously responsible for its own active interpellations. Or, as Butler puts it: "In such a case, the subject is neither a sovereign agent with a purely instrumental relation to language, nor a mere

---

27   Cf. Butler (1997), p. 24f.
28   Cf. Butler (1997), p. 25.
29   Cf. Butler (1997), p. 32.

effect whose agency is pure complicity with prior operations of power."[30] Since language produces concrete consequences for and also in the body, and simultaneously is a living entity over which the individual has control, one can conclude that Butler's theory leads to an interesting question regarding the individual agency when consciously naming and labelling bodies. Although each individual action of naming and labelling bodies is situated in a particular social environment, language is not a fixed or static system, but a living entity that is open to change. As such, individual actions of naming can potentially become a field were individuals can play, improvise and experiment with the creation of alternative ways of naming and labelling bodies.

In the general social context, and especially in the gender topic Butler refers to in her theory, realizing individual agency by experimenting with alternative names and labels might be challenging. As Butler states, the names and labels attached to bodies become stable and powerful through years of constant citation[31], and therefore, on a practical level, alterations might be difficult to realize. However, in my opinion, when researching on individual agency, the artistic research process as a grey zone between discourse and practice[32] offers a wider range of individual agency. In comparison to the social context, where names and labels are rather static, the artistic research context allows for experimenting with most diverse labels and names that are attached to bodies temporarily. It is this temporary state that facilitates artists to play and experiment with unfamiliar names and labels, and, by doing so, producing concrete effects in the body.

In the next chapter, I will turn to the practical perspective. Here, I will reflect on how unfamiliar descriptions and labels were used to affect the internal body image of the performers. Based on this, I will also reflect on where in the artistic research process the power of language to produce concrete effects on the performers' bodies came to its limits.

---

30   Butler (1997), p. 26.
31   Cf. Butler (1993), p. 2.
32   Cf. Hewitt (2005), p. 15.

4.5 Artistic experiments: Appropriating unfamiliar body descriptions

Image: Stach, Jiri (1980) Krajina c.76. Cf. https://www.jiristach.cz/en/photos-80ies.php (date accessed 9 February 2022)

Experiment:
Take 10 minutes to look at the body in the picture above and, while doing so, continuously note down everything and anything you spontaneously notice in or about this body. Keep writing for 10 minutes without ever stopping, and note down whatever comes to mind.

Text excerpts:

Reinartz: The fullness of your breasts is the first thing you offer to anyone taking an interest in you. You are the fruit, the anonymized fruit. You are not a human being, but de-personified sex, mere body, without will or presence. You are ... and violence against yourself. You are not in any way dwarfed by the violence you are experiencing. You stand secure on your legs, even though you are sitting. You offer the fight, you submit to maintain your power, you are a work of art.

Roggan: wrapped in texture, having been sat down and staying upright, I do not see anything, nor do I hear you, I can feel the dark, I feel warm and expectant, your punishment, love, staying away, then I sit there, hour after hour, covering myself, half liberated, blowing the offer into the empty space, what unites us is blindness because we only see separation, and because it is only through darkness that we begin to see we triggered through this game, I almost see the drapery, smell yesterday's sweat, and the high-heeled shoe has made the blisters crack open, piled up, I am forced to remain, sitting, waiting.

Looking at the texts above, one can state that the subjective body descriptions generated in the experiments of the artistic research process were linked to an already existing discourse on BDSM[33] practices, which led us to associating the topics of dominance and submission typical of this context, and categorizing the body as a sexualized body or a body of lust.

Reading the subjective body descriptions, one can notice that there are two levels of description: on the one hand, there are descriptions on the outward physical appearance, i.e. a head separated from the rest of the body by being wrapped closely in cloth, a high-heeled shoe that has made the blisters come open, etc. On the other hand, there are also imaginative and associative labels and descriptions, such as anonymized fruit, tentacles of lust, the offer for a fight, etc. In comparison to the "more neutral" descriptions that can be directly visually perceived when looking at the body on the photo, the imaginative and associative descriptions and categories often subjectively added features to the

---

33   BDSM is a variety of often erotic practices or role play involving bondage, discipline, dominance, and submission.

body.[34] What was created here on a subjective level were body descriptions or categories that were rather metaphorical or surrealistic.

In the following, I will reflect on three different processes of physically appropriating a particular score that was generated in our artistic research process in relation to the "LIZ body"[35]. By reflecting on the insights of those experiments, I will discuss to what extent the physical appropriation of unfamiliar or even fictitious labels and descriptions offers a chance to physically experience yet unknown interests and imaginations regarding the own body. The particular score, the experiments were based on was:

> Anonymized fruit // a body without a face // body orifices // hands // fingers, tentacles of lust // a body of lust. (time frame: 20 minutes)

Process of appropriation 1

The first performer working on the score above was Johanna Roggan. Already in the preceding experiment of subjectively perceiving and describing the LIZ body, Roggan uttered that she felt a strong distance to the body described by her. She described the depicted body in a rather poetical way: as a waiting, helpless, and therefore also vulnerable and exposed body. In the case of the LIZ body, this subjectively felt and described distance between the performer and the body was created less by the body's physical materiality, but rather by Roggan's difficulty at identifying with the body emotionally.

During the entire experiment, Roggan had difficulties to develop an interest for that particular body and the particular descriptions and categories that derived from it, so that, after a while, she experienced boredom while performing the score. Also, after reflecting on different performative tools that could

---

34 In this context, it is interesting how Hubert Sowa describes the relation between observation and the imaginative process. According to Sowa, during the process of observing a picture, the observer's imagination turns to the gaps and the blanks in a picture and individually fills them in. Sowa defines imagination as something that, on the one hand, is closely linked to the skill of perception, and at the same time transcends that perception. In this sense, Sowa defines imagination as receptive, reproductive as well as productive. Cf. Sowa, Hubert (2012) Imagination im Bildungsprozess. In: Sowa Hubert (ed.) Bildung der Imagination. Band 1

35 The name Liz came up in the experiments of individually perceiving and describing the body shown on the image. When reflecting on the individual texts in the research team, the name was intuitively used by several individuals in the group and in the following, whenever a group member referred to this body, it was called the LIZ Body.

be used to translate the descriptions into movement,[36] Roggan did not find an entrance to the physical appropriation of the score. In the reflection on the experiment, Roggan uttered her discomfort with the score by stating that, on a subjective level, she felt an emotional resistance to identify with the body as well as with the created descriptions and labels. Within the reflection, she assumed that this emotional resistance made it difficult for her to step into a performative attitude in which she would be able to play with the performative translations of the descriptions.

As the director of this research project, the question I was suddenly confronted with was whether I wasn't actually forcing something on Roggan by expecting her to appropriate those categories derived from the depicted LIZ body through performative strategies. In the context of a production, a situation like this would create a question of hierarchy and possible use of power. As a choreographer, I would then have to accept the personal preferences of the performer or, alternatively, the performer would have to find a way of succumbing, despite her inner resistance and lack of interest, to the given task. In the context of this artistic research, with its focus on exploring strategies of consciously recreating the own individual body image, it surely would not have made sense to force the appropriation of unfamiliar physical categories on Roggan.

What this example clearly showed was that the power of language to produce concrete effects in the performer's body arrived at its limits the moment the performer inwardly objected to the depicted body and the descriptions and categories developed from it. Thinking Roggan's experiment further, it can therefore be concluded that the prerequisite for the appropriation of descriptions and labels connected with a body that is individually perceived as unfamiliar is the performer's will and emotional openness to temporarily identify with them.

Process of appropriation 2

The second performer that worked with the score and the related LIZ body was Juli Reinartz. In her performative appropriation, Reinartz focused in particular on three details from the descriptions: orifices, tentacles of lust, and anonymized fruit. Reinartz's choice of the detail of orifices in connection with the LIZ body came as a surprise, since in the original photo not a single orifice

---

36   Also cf. chapter 3 – On Methods, p. 60f.

was visible but they were all covered by a large cloth. Interestingly, in her experiment of appropriation, Reinartz occupied herself most intensely with the mouth and thus had chosen exactly the one orifice and erogenous zone that was completely covered in the photo. With the help of the method of inner focussing[37], Reinartz tackled the detail of body orifices mentioned in the descriptions in such a way that she developed a playful examination of the motor level and sensual level of the mouth.

In contrast to that, the two other details from the descriptions, i.e. "tentacles of lust" and "anonymized fruit", at first also produced an irritation in Reinartz's process of appropriation – since, naturally, concrete physical counterparts did not and could not exist. Yet, in contrast to Roggan, Reinartz developed an acute interest in examining those details in the course of her process of appropriation. In her experiment Reinartz could bridge the gap between her own body and those unfamiliar and, to a certain extent, also fictitious categories by using her imagination.

This process of imagination did not take place intellectually, but in her performative activity. To be able to carry out her performative appropriation of the descriptions, Reinartz challenged herself by asking herself several questions: What could, for example, fingers do, when used as tentacles of lust? How could they move? What could they make contact with? What other ideas and emotions come up if one imagines the body as an anonymized fruit? What kind of movement and what kind of presence does this imagination invite?

Connecting the individual experiences from the artistic research process with Butler's theory of body construction through labeling, one difference becomes apparent: While Butler considers language to be mainly a tool for power that suppresses the body's versatility, in the artistic experiments, labeling the body through language was used for a different purpose. For our artistic experiments, language was a tool to define unfamiliar potential physical states, even if the body had not realized and experienced them before.

During Reinartz's experiments, the physical appropriation of the unfamiliar body category "tentacles of lust" implied an imagination of the fingers as tentacles of lust. This, in Reinartz's case, so far unfamiliar imagination, in turn, affected Reinartz's individual perception of her fingers. In the context of the experiment, Reinartz no longer perceived her hands as tools for holding or touching something, but she perceived them as something that can perceive lust.

---

37 Also cf. p. 60 of this paper.

4. The first artistic research project "The bodies we are" 87

Reinartz used this new perspective to develop alternative specific finger movements and gestures. In the course of the experiment, those movements gradually converged, among others, on the topic of "receiving and sending", which was explored further in the movement research.

When reflecting on the subjective experience after the experiment, Reinartz stated that, in the course of the experiment, she perceived her body as a physical space or vessel into which she was able to invite anything mystical, anything evil, or the weird. Relating Reinartz's individual experiences to Gallagher's concept of the body image as something that is built through perceptual experiences, emotional attitude, and conceptual construction, one can describe Reinartz's experiment as a process of playfully constructing a temporal body image. In this process, the particular way of labeling the body was used to generate alternative imaginations regarding the body which were then physically explored and experienced.

Process of appropriation 3

The third performer working with the score "an anonymized fruit, a body without a face, body orifices, hands, fingers, tentacles of lust, a body of lust" was Vania Rovisco. In contrast to Roggan and Reinartz, Rovisco explicitly mentioned her interest in the depicted LIZ body and its subsequent body descriptions well before she actually experimented with their appropriation. Her interest was derived from the topic of the body of lust, in the context of which she considered submission as a conscious use of power. Unlike Roggan and Reinartz, Rovisco used also an additional tool in her experiment, which was a microphone.[38]

During her experiment, Rovisco at first concentrated on the physical appropriation of the described categories of "body of lust" in combination with "body without a face". Here, she experimented with various gestures concerning the "body of lust", such as, for example, "hand on vulva" or "hand slides into the trousers", and at the same time she experimented with her face being visible or invisible to the observers. With regard to the description of "body without face", Rovisco focused on the performative relationship with the observers of the experiment. In this regard, she experimented with turning her face away from the observers as well as withdrawing her glance so far inside herself that

---

38   The choice of using a microphone was not planned beforehand. The microphone was in the dance studio we worked in and Rovisco spontaneously took it during the experiment.

in the end her glance, though visible, in my experience, seemed to be disappearing into her altogether.

Through this alternating between presence and absence of her face during her experiments, Rovisco created a performative play on closeness versus distance created a tension. Through this performative play, I was confronted with various questions concerning my own role as observer: At this moment, who is in a position to observe whose body? And who has the power to actually withdraw from that observing gaze? As a spectator of the experiment, I was left with a feeling of insecurity concerning those questions, since, through the performative experiment, I was confronted with a body that, despite its plain visibility, was capable of withdrawing to a certain extent from my observing gaze.

Although Rovisco's face was not covered by anything during the experiment and was therefore basically present, I, as the observer, at various moments in the performative experiment did not perceive a human face anymore. Instead of Rovisco's human face, I felt confronted with an uneven surface with a dark, huge, breathing hole, with the surface simply appearing to be part of an object-like body. The hand simultaneously sliding into the trousers triggered associations of autoerotic activities, thus redirecting my perception of that body towards perceiving a subject again, rather than an object as before. In Rovisco's experiment, her particular way of appropriating the descriptions of "body without face" in relation to a "body of lust" led to me, as an observer, perceiving her body as object as well as subject at the same time. The simultaneousness of those physical states triggered various moments of irritation, since it was impossible for me to categorize the observed body during that experiment.

Did I now see a body that, by temporarily extinguishing its own face for the duration of the performative experiment, had voluntarily rendered itself into a non-human object? Or did I see a subject that was performing autoerotic gestures and activities and that could actively vanish from an outside observer's intrusive gaze? Or was a new potential body image created in those moments of irritation, such as, for example, that of an independent, self-satisfied object of lust?

Reflecting on this irritation that I felt when observing the experiment, one can state that the physical appropriation of the score not only had an impact on Rovisco's internal body- and self-perception, but it also had a radical impact on how Rovisco's body was perceived from the external perspective of the observer.

4. The first artistic research project "The bodies we are"   91

In Rovisco's internal perception of the experiment, similar to what occurred in Reinartz's experiment, different physical topics evolved that went beyond the initially appropriated verbal descriptions. In Rovisco's case, they implied an inner focus on the mouth/anus connection and a conscious playing with her breathing. Partly with and partly without amplification through a microphone, Rovisco played in her experiment with different degrees of audibility of her long and expressive breaths, which kept growing louder and louder and taking up more and more space as well as attention. This is how the play on closeness and distance was intensified further, which made it difficult for me as an observer to distance myself from this body. This way, and in the course of the experiment, Rovisco created a body image that alternated between the states of subject or object, presence and absence, abandonment and (self-)control.

This particular body image that was created by Rovisco, escaped any exact definition since the performer created a simultaneity of different, partly even contradictory bodily actions, qualities and intentions. In order to approach this created body images from a different perspective, I set up an additional experiment: I asked Rovisco to keep on playing with her performative actions, while additionally using language in order to articulate all imaginations and desires that might come up during her physical and performative exploration.

Text excerpt from Rovisco's experiment:

> "I imagine I am a filter of thoughts, that I am a permission. I imagine that my breath goes through the space, enters your mouth and exits through your anus. I imagine not knowing. I imagine walking through the streets looking out through my asshole. I imagine throwing you against the wall. I imagine that you become a new you. I imagine to accept. I imagine that your odour is so intense that everybody leaves the room. I imagine that I am a tunnel with no exit that you enter. I imagine that I am a hole that you dig and I put myself in. I imagine that I am the waste in your intestine. I imagine that my breath becomes your thoughts. I imagine that you take these thoughts and that you shove them up your anus and that they become my breath. I imagine that there are thousands like me surrounding you, that you come inside me and that you ejaculate through my eyes."[39]

---

39   The text is a transcript of a spoken text that Rovisco improvised in the experiment.

In the reflection on the experiment within the research team, the question to whom this "I" in "I imagine" belonged arose. When asking Rovisco about her individual relation or identification with the articulated imaginations, she stated that she personally would not be at all interested in her own personal individual imaginations. Instead, she would be interested in the generated experiences themselves. Thus, Rovisco considered the uttered imaginations not as something belonging to her personally, but she considered them as a result of the particular physical and sensuous experience she had had during the experiment. Thinking Rovisco's answer further, one could consider the desires that were articulated in the experiment as fictitious, but at the same time rooted in Rovisco's real physical experience of her individual body.

Therefore, one might consider that Rovisco's process of appropriation not only constitutes a potential leap to a different space of action and perception, but also a potential leap to different imaginations and desires with which the subject is not forced to automatically identify. This is why one might comprehend the appropriation of other, unfamiliar body descriptions and labels as a method of distancing oneself from what is individual and subjective, as a strategy to push the own limits, as a camouflage tactic, or as opposition to a body as "identity project".

Making a connection between the artistic experiments and the neoliberal social context with its values of enhancement and control, one can state that the performative context of the experiments created a temporal freedom in which the body could be considered as a field for experimentation. By proposing that the body, at least in the performative context, must not necessarily be considered as something that is supposed to express the individual self, the individual relationship with the own body could be rather experimental – not in the sense that the performers did not care about the own physical body, but in a way that the attitude to the own body was characterized by a radical openness, accompanied with an individual interest in also exploring the devious, absurd, or fragile potentials of the own body.

In the next chapter, I will change perspective and enter into the field of theory in order to discuss the specific temporal relationship between sensory perception and processes of describing and labeling. Here, I will focus on the gap between the two fields and discuss it as a creative potential in the process of consciously recreating body images.

4.6 Theoretical perspective: The creative gap between sensory perception and processes of naming

In the first chapter of his book "The Phenomenology of Mind"[40], Hegel discusses the particular relationship between language and sensory perception. In his theory, Hegel – unlike Merleau-Ponty and Butler – is not particularly interested in how the body or a body image is constructed. Instead, he puts his focus on the particular knowledge that can be gained from experiencing something through the senses. This is also where the particular relationship between sensory perception and language plays an important role. Since Hegel's thoughts can also be applied to my artistic research on consciously recreating body images, I will, in the following, briefly summarize Hegel's findings.

Hegel points out that any perception of an object – such as the body – can only be a temporary thing, since what is perceived potentially changes at any moment, depending on who perceives it and when and where. Therefore, according to Hegel, sense-certainty, i.e., certainty with regard to perception, is limited to a stable (self-identical) relationship between the perceiving subject and the perceived object. So the question is: What happens if the perceiving subject wants to share his or her perception with someone outside this self-identical relationship?

According to Hegel, at that moment, the perceiving subject has to point out what he or she means. At that moment language, in its mediating function, becomes involved.[41] The necessity of using language in order to point out what one is perceiving leads to the following situation: When the perceiving subject wants to share his or her sensory perception (of the body or any other object) with someone else, the perceiving individual has to point out a "Now" and claim this Now to be a truth. However, at the moment of communication, this Now has already passed. What the subject has to do, then, is to cancel this first truth and point out the Now as something that has been – but what has been is not now. Therefore, the subject also has to cancel that truth and has to point out a new and thus different Now.[42]

According to Hegel, one can deduce two basic characteristics with regard to the relationship between language and sensory perception: Firstly, when de-

---

[40] Hegel (2003)
[41] Cf. Hegel (2003), p. 59.
[42] Cf. Hegel (2003), p. 59f.

scribing sensory perception (of the own or another particular body), language can never occur simultaneously with the moment of perception, and that is why it never represents the very moment that is meant and perceived by an individual. Therefore, what an individual perceives and "means" is never identical to how an individual expresses that perception and content. Secondly, language is not only late, but it also transforms the "meaning" of the perceived object into something universal which can be approached by more than one individual. Therefore, any label or description is freezing a particular Here and Now and ignores the constant transformation of the Here and Now. That is why Hegel concludes that both sensory perception and processes of naming already include their potential negation and transformation as integral parts.[43]

Since Hegel focuses on the question of sense certainty, he considers the constant transformation of sensory perception and also the problem of naming it to be a dilemma.[44] To escape this dilemma, he proposes to point out any object of perception as a temporary truth, which also means having to witness and accept a constant process of negation and transformation.

What can be derived from Hegel's thoughts with regard to my artistic research process? If body images are generated by movement and individual perception on the one hand, and verbal description on the other, Hegel's experiments clarify that any descriptions of a perceived body can never be 'up-to-date' since, for one thing, they take place only after a certain minimal delay in time and, for another, language transforms the subjective perception into something universal, which always entails a transformation.

Once the aim of one's research – unlike Hegel's – is not arriving at certainty when it comes to sensory perception, the gaps and transformations resulting from physical experience and description of the body not overlapping completely will turn into an interesting potential. If language that is used to describe a body always leaves a gap, this discordance could also be considered as an interesting chance to push at the limits of how a body is perceived in a particular moment, with regard to how a body might be perceived in a future moment. In this regard, one could understand the gap between sensory perception of a body and its verbal description as a productive contrast between possible present and future perceptions of the body.

In my artistic research process, I considered the gap as a creative potential with which one could actively play. A similar perspective on the gap between

---

43 Cf. Hegel (2003), p. 60.
44 Cf. Hegel (2003), p. 60f.

sensory perception and processes of describing and labeling can be found in Schiller's book "On the Aesthetic Education of Man".[45] Based on the assumption that the human individual has a twofold nature which consists of a sensuous part and a intelligible part, Schiller states that there are two forces working in the individual.[46] The first one is called the sensuous impulse, which is connected to sensory perception and aims at mutation and alteration.[47] The second one is called the formal impulse, which is connected to language and reason making, and aims at giving the individual freedom (agency)[48], since it can be used to structure the diversity of one's sensory perceptions.[49]

According to Schiller, both impulses can mutually act and react upon each other. Based on this assumption, Schiller considers the play impulse as a third force[50] which enables a playful interaction between the sensuous and the intelligible part of the individual. Here, play is considered as an inner-subjective capacity of playing with the own cognitive power.[51] Thus, the play impulse creates a temporally limited experience of freedom for the individual where it can alter its own perception by playing with its way of thinking, and, vice versa, alter its way of thinking by playing with its way of perceiving things. Combining formal and sensuous impulse, the play impulse suspends the antagonism between the sensuous and the intelligible part of the individual and replaces it with a dynamic interaction between both. In this understanding, play is everything that is neither subjectively or objectively contingent, and yet imposes neither outward nor inward necessity.[52] In Schiller's understanding, the play impulse aims at reconciling becoming with absolute being, and variation with identity.[53]

---

45   Schiller (2014)
46   Cf. Schiller (2014), p. 50ff.
47   Cf. Schiller (2014), p. 51.
48   From today's perspective, Schiller's equation of freedom with the rational impulse of the individual is surely problematic. As discourse analysis has shown, every process of thought production is already situated in social discourses, which implies particular norms and values. As Villa points out, those discourses are not fixed, but they can be influenced by alternative discourse production. Cf. Villa (2008b), p. 267. Cf. also p. 37ff. of this paper. In this context, one could understand Schiller's concept of freedom in terms of agency of the subject.
49   Cf. Schiller (2014), p. 52.
50   Cf. Schiller (2014), p. 59.
51   Cf Neuenfeld (2005), p. 14.
52   Cf. Schiller (2014), p. 62.
53   Cf. Schiller (2014), p. 59.

Applying Schiller's understanding of play on Gallagher's concept of the body image that combines both sensory perception and processes of naming and labeling through language, one can conclude that the body image could also be considered as a potential playground. By understanding the mutual influence between sensory perception and thinking process and, vice versa, conceiving processes of naming and labeling as something that can influence perception, in the context of this research, I considered the re-creation of the body image as a potential field for playfully creating yet unfamiliar temporal versions of the own self. Therefore, the bodies of the performers were not considered as something exclusively personal, but as a place where the performers could play and experiment with the temporal construction of yet unknown and even fictitious versions of their own selves.

Within the research process, this attitude toward the body led to several questions: Once one no longer defines the body as a place for individual self-expression, what alternative perspectives on the body might be suggested? In other words, what function might the body fulfill once one looks upon it as something not exclusively personal? In the course of our artistic research project those questions led to another question: Could a body image also be understood as a fictitious "role[54]" one might appropriate? This thought triggered an interest in a particular American approach of play-acting called Method Acting. Method Acting is best known for its method of appropriating fictitious roles via a "real" sensory and emotional experience.

4.7 Artistic experiments: Appropriating an unfamiliar method. The body image as a role in Method Acting

It is precisely because not a single member of the research team had been educated in the field of Method Acting that I became interested in an attempt at appropriating that method for my research project. I have labelled this attempt an appropriation of a method since I applied strategies from a different method to my own field of research. Since I was not educated in Method Acting, my particular approach to the method was rather selective and experimental.

---

54 In the context of this work, I consider a role as a foreign, fictitious character experienced inside the actor's own body as real, physically as well as emotionally. Cf. Morris, Eric (1998) Acting, Imaging and the Unconscious, p. 9.

In appropriating specific tools from Method Acting, my interest lay in exploring an alternative perspective on the body as a place and medium to perform a fictitious role, i.e., a fictive character with a fictitious past and future.

In my preparations for the experiment, I worked with two books – Eric Morris' "Acting, Imaging and the Unconscious"[55] and Susan Batson's "Truth"[56]. Morris' practical manual for actors makes it clear that Method Acting, a method originally developed by Konstantin Stanislawski and Lee Strasberg and later modified by Morris himself, defines an actor's appropriation of a fictitious role as "becoming the character", a definition that entails considering the actor to be a "professional experiencer"[57]. It is in this sense that the role in Method Acting is looked upon as a foreign, fictional character experienced as physically and emotionally real inside the actor's own body. This "becoming the character" expects from the actor to totally immerse himself in the emotional and sensory perceptions of that particular role.

In order to enable the actor to do so, Morris applies two strategies that are closely connected in practice. The first strategy is based on the assumption central to Method Acting that sensory perception can be deceived with the help of imaging, and can consequently be transformed into sensory perceptions that are felt to be real. The second strategy aims at making the actor identify emotionally with the fictional role, so that this will generate affects and emotions that the actor experiences as "real". In the context of emotional identification with the fictitious role, Susan Batson's development of the method goes even further into detail.

According to Batson, there are two layers of an individual and therefore also of a role; an outer layer of identity, which she calls a "Public Persona", and an inner layer of identity, which she calls a "Need".[58] With her concept of the Public Persona, Batson refers to the Persona concept of psychoanalyst Carl Gustav Jung. According to Jung, every individual creates and maintains a persona. This persona could also be considered to be a mask that one wears in public with the purpose of hiding the inner self. Batson calls this inner self the Need. In her concept of the Need, Batson also refers to psychoanalysis, not in a scientific way, but rather by using the idea of an unresolved conflict and unfulfilled

---

55 Morris (1998)
56 Batson, Susan (2007) TRUTH, personas, needs and flaws in building actors and creating characters.
57 Cf. Morris (1998), S.9.
58 Cf. Batson (2007), p. 31.

emotional desire that unconsciously motivates all actions and choices of a person.[59]

My particular interest to appropriate, with the help of the Method Acting technique, some of the depicted bodies collected in the artistic research process as a role therefore confronted me with the following question: What sensory perceptions, which Public Persona, and what Needs might the depicted bodies on the collected photos and images imply? This question, in turn, confronted me with the subsequent problem that the collected photos of bodies in the research process did not imply fictitious narratives in the sense of a film script, which then Public Persona and Need could be derived from. However, having generated plenty of individual descriptions of those photographed bodies, there was fictitious material which could be used to deduce at least fragmentary information, concerning the fields of sensory perception, a possible Public Persona, and a possible emotional Need.

To develop sensory experiences in a fictitious role, Morris applies the following strategy: From among a number of categories (time and place, relationships, emotional state, character, connection to the particular time in history, topic, and sub-text), he first selects those categories that, in his opinion, are relevant to the particular role in question. In a second step, the actor adds something to this particular choice that stems from his own archive of experiences. This may take the form of an object, a person, or a place that, in the actor's personal view, indicates a parallel to the role she or he has been assigned.

After this preparation, the process of asking questions begins. With regard to the aspects chosen, it investigates what the physical, sensory, and also the emotional perceptions of the assigned role are. What is interesting about Morris' particular technique of imaging is his shifting from the macro level to the micro level. In this process, the questions asked refer to continuously more specific details while, at the same time, addressing all the senses simultaneously, i.e., seeing, hearing, smelling, tasting, and feeling through touching. All of those senses are expected to be linked back to the emotional level. The actor might be asked: What time of day is it?, Where are you?, What are you seeing?, What colors and structures are you seeing?, What are you hearing?, Are you alone or are you with others?, How are you feeling?, What would you like most to be doing now?, What is the temperature (like)?, What can you smell?, What smells do you notice?, What is the smell, exactly?, What other smells are mixed

---

59   Cf. Batson (2007), p. 32.

in with the central/dominant smell?, What feelings are evoked by the smell?, etc.

The sample questions listed above show how Morris combines questions concerning the physical internal proprioception with those concerning the perception of the external surrounding space. What is interesting – and central to Method Acting – is the strong focus on specific emotions that have been generated through a particular sensory perception. Looking at Morris' method from the perspective of Gallagher's concept of the body image, one will notice that Morris' method links up with all three of the areas that the body image is compiled from, namely sensory perception, conceptualization through language, and the emotional level. Morris' method of combining verbal questions with verbal answers, which the actor is expected to experience both sensually and emotionally, leads to the construction of an entirely fictitious, yet at the same time truly felt and experienced internal and external world. This makes it possible for the actor to transform the fictional role into real physical and emotional experiences. Thus, in Method Acting, the appropriation of an unfamiliar role also constitutes an empathic process that requires emotional identification with an unfamiliar emotional Need.

Comparing the use of language in Method Acting to the particular way language is often used in the Contemporary Dance context, one can state several differences. In Method Acting, language is used in the rehearsal situation to immediately express internal sensations and emotions. Those internal sensations and emotions, in turn, belong to a fictional role with a fictitious past and future that is situated in a narrative context with a (mostly) linear story line. In the contemporary dance context, individual sensations and emotions while working on choreographic material must not necessarily be articulated on a verbal level and if so, this verbal articulation more often happens afterwards in reflection talks.[60]

In the Contemporary Dance context, creating movement material with the body in the choreographic process is, in most cases, not related to a narrative storyline that entails a fictitious past and future of the dancing body. In the choreographic context, the body is rather understood as a medium and place for performing, experiencing and exploring movement. The particular choreographic strategies to generate movement can be very diverse, working with abstract forms and structures, exploring a social or individual topic related to the

---

60 Also cf. p. 43f. of this paper. As the dance field is highly diverse, surely there are plenty of exceptions to this general observation.

body, exploring emotional states, just to name a few. It was exactly this other, for me unfamiliar perspective on the body as a carrier of a fictitious role, with a fictitious past and future, that I wanted to investigate in the research on the Method-Acting approach.

In the following, I will reflect on a Method Acting experiment that took place in the practical research process. The experiment was based on the picture below, as well as on the written descriptions of that body.

Image: Kahn, Brian (creative director) & LHGFX (photography) BODIES OF WORK. Vol.1. Cf. https://www.bodybuilding.com/fun/bodies-of-work.html (date accessed 9 February 2022)

Text excerpts from the written descriptions:

Roggan: flat stomach, blood, sweat, tensed muscles around the mouth, being at the center, muscles, testosterone, shoulders (pulled) back so that the chest will appear to be wider, work without discipline, painlessness, the minor materiality of the body, lips, shaven chest, I fuck noisily, brute force and beauty, childhood days.

Velsinger: muscle mass that is meant to be visible, demonstration of power, form is important, between the insides of the hands counter pressure is building up, hands as penis, strength without a goal, muscular optics, distancing oneself from function, body is meant to be massive, a steeled body, masculine ideal of beauty, having a bull's neck, concentrated feeding stuff and protein to grow muscular mass, veins stand out, sixpack, protective armor, the muscles are your armor, an armor without a battle, a battle without a purpose, training practice, a surplus of energy, being prepared, being potent and potentially capable of whatever, a display of muscles, the battle is taking place somewhere else.

Based on the particular photo of a male bodybuilder and on the particular written descriptions of that body, I pooled all the information I had at my disposal for the role that was supposed to be appropriated. From that pool, Reinartz chose the following categories that, in her view, were central with regard to that role – topic: "presentation", place: "always stand right in the middle of a background", time: "repeat something over and over", need: "wanting to be seen and appreciated". Those criteria were the base from which Reinartz started her first performative experiment, during which Roggan and I took over the task of asking the questions while Reinartz answered them out loud.

Excerpt from Reinartz's answers:

> "It is stuffy in here. I can smell yesterday's smoke. I'm in a room somewhere in the basement of some building. A competition is taking place. I'm presenting my body. There are not many people here to watch. My neck is tensed up, my view is restricted, to my right and to my left everything is blurred. I can feel a pressure in my chest, I'm feeling insecure, somewhat lonely. (...)"[61]

Reflecting on Reinartz's verbal answers to our questions, one can state that Reinartz produced a fictitious narrative situation. This situation propelled the emotional sensation to the foreground. As a result of this focus on emotional sensation, which one might label as the fear of failing or as the need to achieve something in order to be recognized etc., Reinartz's experiment turned out to be very different from the ones before that had their focus more on physical sensation. The narrative emotional

---

61   The text is a transcript of a spoken text that Reinartz improvised in the experiment.

situation made it easier for the actual performer as well as the observers to feel empathy, which, in turn, led to a noticeable decrease of the initial feeling of extreme distance toward the body on the photo and the descriptions derived from it. This is how the image of the male body-builder's body, initially perceived by everyone on the team with derision and distance, could, in the course of the experiment, become a kind of foil to mirror one's own striving for achievement and recognition.

Yet, at the same time, it became obvious during the experiment that Reinartz was struggling to generate physical movement in line with her verbal responses. Due to the focus on the verbal assertions and on the narrative level thus created, the impression developed that the actual act of speaking was partly obstructing the direct physical movement and, therefore, also the direct physical experiencing. When making a connection between this problem area and, on the other hand, Hegel's thesis that there is a time-lag as well as transformation between sensory perception and verbalization, then one will notice the challenge in this method. The answers expressed in words cannot fully overlap with one's own physical and emotional perception, and therefore function more as an assertion.

However, in the practical experiment, this problem produced a frustration in Reinartz. When reflecting on that frustration after the experiment, Reinartz stated that, during the experiment, she had a recurring feeling that she was giving only a "make-believe" performance on the physical level, since, in her internal perception, she could not fully relate to her performed movements and actions. Relating Reinartz's frustration with Schiller's concept of play, in which the sensuous impulse and the formal impulse can mutually influence each other, once could state that Reinartz was not fully able to enter into the mode of playing. One reason for this phenomenon might be a lack of practice, since Reinartz, in her artistic practice as choreographer and performer, had rarely worked with the immediate verbalization of physical sensations and imagination. Another reason for the difficulties might have been that, in Method Acting, performing a role is closely linked to a concrete and linear narrative structure. As stated above, working with a such a narrative is rather unusual in the contemporary choreographic field, where narrative structures are mostly used in a more open and fragmented way. This difference could also be a possible reason why, in Reinartz's internal perception, the uttering of her sentences felt rather unfamiliar and partly even irritating.

Despite the difficulties that arose during the Method Acting experiment, the experiment added two crucial, previously unrepresented aspects to the artistic research on re-creating the own body image to initiate unfamiliar body- and self-perceptions. The first aspect is the potential of using language as a tool for adding a fictitious past and future to the individual body, and the second is the focus on the level of emotional identification with another body. This is why, despite all difficulties with Method Acting, this experiment evoked an interest in the potential of the body as the place where emotions can be experienced and expressed, yet where the borderline between one's own emotions and the unfamiliar and even fictitious ones is blurred.[62]

During the research process, this interest led to the question whether Method Acting might not also be appropriated in a different way, in which the physical level of movement could take up more space. In consequence, we combined the Method-Acting technique of asking questions with a particular exercise from "Action Theater[63]". The original exercise from "Action Theater" was to switch and translate between the three layers "shape", "sensation" and "action". In our experiment, we added the two additional layers "setting" and "need" to the exercise and combined it with the particular question technique of method acting. The starting point of the following experiment were, again, the photo of the male body-builder as well as the descriptions of this body as generated in the course of the research process.

The overall task of the performative experiment was to continuously switch and translate between five performative layers. Each layer was connected to a different focus as well as to a different performative task. The changes between the layers were announced from the outside perspective of observing and witnessing the experiment. When changing, the task was to individually translate one layer into the next layer. The five layers were: 1. "Shape" in the sense of a created posture. 2. "Sensation" in the sense of perceiving the body on the sensuous level. 3. "Action" in the sense of creating physical movement. 4. "Setting" in the sense of using imagination to create a fictitious environment the moving

---

62 Whether the reasons for our difficulties were my own or the co-researchers' limited expertise with regard to Method Acting, or whether they stemmed from the continuous "disruption" between language and sensory perception, cannot be answered conclusively. To be able to decide here, one would have to hire a professional Method Acting coach to conduct the experiment.

63 Action theater is an improvisational physical theater training and performance method, created by the American performance artist and director Ruth Zapora, which aims at integrating movement, vocalization, and speech. Cf. Zapora, Ruth (1995), Action Theater: The Improvisation of Presence. Or also: Zapora, Ruth (2014) Improvisation On the Edge: Notes from On and Off the Stage.

body is situated in, including concrete narrations taking place. 5. "Need", in the sense of possible desires and emotions, subjectively perceived during the concrete physical experiencing. On levels 1–3 the performers only used movement. On levels 4 and 5, the performers used also language to verbally articulate the upcoming imaginations and associated desires and interests.

Text excerpt from the verbal instructions of the experiment from the outside perspective[64]:

> Find a shape that you associate with the body in the picture. Now change over to sensation. What do you feel when inside this shape? Which of the senses are relevant now? (...) intensify this. (...). Now change over to a setting. Imagine that setting as precisely as possible. Where are you? Who is there with you? What are you saying? Who are you saying that to? What are you doing? Are you moving, if so, what does your movement look like? Is there a smell? (...) Then change over to Need: What emotions are you feeling? What is your interest or desire now? What are you looking for? Then change over to shape again. So now transform your entire need into one single shape. What shape has the need taken? Choose from it. Change again if you feel that this is not yet the shape that fully represents the need. (...) Then change over to action. What is this form like in an action? Extend this action to its maximum. Then reduce it to its minimum. What parts of your body are taking part in your action? What is the quality of your moving like? What are your directions in space? And then back to need again: What feelings and desires concerning your body does your movement generate? What feeling can you sense in your body right now? What would you like to do now? And now for sensation: What does your body feel like at the moment? Which parts of your body do you actually feel? Which senses are aware at the moment? Move more deeply into your sensations, forget everything else, simply concentrate on what you are physically experiencing at the moment. Transform this sensation into a setting. (...) etc.

---

64 Based on the method of perpetually changing from one of the five levels over to another, the process of development is improvised spontaneously by the person giving the instructions. Therefore, the text excerpt at hand is simply one example.

4. The first artistic research project "The bodies we are" 107

4. The first artistic research project "The bodies we are" 109

The continuous processes of translation and all the changes between the five different levels made it possible to generate during the experiment not only a variety of non-verbal postures, actions, and sensory perceptions, but also verbally as well as non-verbally expressed emotions, desires, and also fictitious narrative situations. A specific physical action like squashing something in turn generated a specific sensory as well as emotional reaction – like, for example, striking physical tautness and aggression. When this sensation was then transformed via language into an emotional need, though, the need mentioned was, for example, to expand and to take more space. Translating this need into a fictitious setting, the scenery of a vast and dry landscape was described, for example, in which a competition was supposed to take place. In this landscape, different bodies were present, exhaustedly moving in space, looking for something. In this scenery the performer imagined the own body as a human battery, etc. The concrete example shows that each layer had an effect on the next one following, yet also that during each transformation the original 'content' was 'updated' with the help of slight shifts away from that content.

Due to our frequent changing of layers it became possible during the experiment to generate complex aspects concerning the appropriated body as a role, aspects that comprised specific shapes, movement material and sensations as well as imagined sceneries in which concrete narrative situations could be generated. In the course of the experiment, those narrative situations became more and more complex, containing fragments of a particular past as well as desires regarding a possible future of the body. In contrast to the first experiment, this experiment allowed for both, generating movement material that was associated with the male-body builder as well as generating concrete narrative situations implying particular relationships with others, particular emotions, needs and interests.

In Rovisco's experiment of transitioning between the 5 different layers, a wide array of performative material between abstract and narrative layers was created. On a movement level, it contained a variety of fight-related gestures, a movement quality oscillating between building up a high level of muscular tension and discharging it through sudden explosive movements by her limbs. Regarding the particular use of space, the performative material included Rovisco's imagination that her body leaves physical and energetic imprints everywhere it moves, in the air or on material that it touched, on other (imagined) bodies, etc.

Transitioning between the five layers of the experiment, Rovisco used language to create several fragmented narratives that were based on the upcoming imagination of her body as a human battery. This body was situated in a vast and dry landscape that only had a limited amount of resources available for all bodies living there. In this scenery, Rovisco imagined her own body as a source which can produce an endless amount of force or physical energy that could not only be used by herself, but also by others. Based on the photo of the male body builder and its descriptions, the experiment enabled Rovisco not only to develop various movement materials, but also different narrative fragments, which were performed and experienced with and in her body.

Taking Rovisco's experiment as an example, one can summarize the results from the appropriation and the individual extension of Method Acting as follows: What can be practiced with Method Acting is to temporarily identify with a body that is perceived as different from the own self. By individually ascribing a particular need to the other body, and by searching for this particular need in the own self, the felt distance between the two bodies might potentially turn into a complicity between both. The complex process of generating physical movements, gestures, sensations, as well as using imagination to generate narrative sceneries with concrete relationships, desires, etc. leads to the creation of a fictitious role that can be physically and emotionally experienced in the body of the performer. By imagining her own body as a source of endless power that can be used by her and also by others, and by adding a fictitious past and future to this body, Rovisco could use her body as a place to experience a temporal state of otherness. This state of otherness is not a complete embodiment of the male body builder but it is the result of temporarily practicing identification with this body. In this process, Rovisco also added new, rather unexpected associations to the initial photo of the body builder, which, in turn, also changed the perspective on that body.

4.8 Conclusion first research project: The body as a sensitive container

Connecting the insights of the first research project "the bodies we are" and the initial interest of this paper to search for alternative perspectives on the body that differ from the neoliberal idea of considering the body as a representative of an ideal self, what could be an alternative proposal?

In the experiments of the research project "the bodies we are", we explored various strategies to use the individual body as a place to become unfamiliar to the own self. This process can be described as creating frictions or confrontations between body images that already existed in the performer's bodies and aspects of other bodies, with which the performers, for individual or social reasons, did not want, could not, or were not allowed to identify. In different experiments, we tried to temporarily bridge this gap by exploring strategies of physically appropriating details of other bodies with which the performers did not identify.

As the artistic experiments have shown, our attempts of exploring the body as a place to become unfamiliar to the own self were not consistently successful. The task to appropriate details of another body which one personally does not want or should not identify with also produced partly defensive reactions in the performers. However, in those moments in which the performers could transform this resistance into an interest and curiosity in the other, it became possible to use the process of appropriation as a chance to playfully experiment with the own individual body images.

This process, in turn, enabled the performers to experience several changes in the own sense of self. For example, they perceived the own body as a massive, excessive, and voluptuous body dreaming about endless lustful expansion. Or as a vessel with several tentacles or antennas which could be used to invite anything mystical, evil, or weird. Or as a body of lust without a human face that alternates between the state of subject and object, and that has the power to actually withdraw from the observing gaze. Or as a human battery that can produce an endless amount of energy for itself and others, etc.

In contrast to the neoliberal interest in working on the body in order to achieve a better version of the own self, the artistic experiments facilitated a rather unintentional and playful use of the body. Based on an individual approval and interest, the body could be used as a place to experiment with and rehearse alternative temporal versions of one's own self with which the performers did not necessarily fully identify.

Connecting those insights to my initial interest in alternative perspectives that differ from the neoliberal understanding of the body as an identity project, I would like to propose to think of the body as a sensitive container which can be actively "filled" with diverse "content" by the individual. By proposing this choreographic working term of the body as a sensitive container, I do not refer to the kind of dead container with standardized measurements that we can see at the harbor. Of course the human body is not literally empty, neither is it standardized and surely the body is not passive, since it gets affected by what is "put in" it.

By labeling the body as a sensitive container, I rather focus on the body's potential openness as a possible carrier of manifold labels, experiences, imaginations and desires. While the social practices of self-optimization radically narrow down how bodies are used and perceived, the proposal of the body as a container puts its focus on exploring yet unknown, unaccepted or unwanted potentials of the body. When I speak about actively and consciously "filling" the body container, I refer to a self-determined process that is based on the subject's approval and interest. Therefore, "filling" the body container with other experiences, perceptions, imaginations, movements, etc. is a process of individual negotiation. Since the body offers the chance to also perceive the own self in such manifold ways, the body container can also be considered as a place for experimentation, while the generated insights might imply yet unknown relationships, desires or interests.

Regarding the relationship with time, one can state that the content of a body as a sensitive container is assembled from two different time levels: the past and the present. The past includes everything that is already "inside" the container, i.e., all the names, labels, experiences, physical practices, emotions, and sensory perceptions, and therefore also all body images that have already exerted an influence on the body. The present, on the other hand, includes all the potential foreign names, categories, and sensory and emotional experiences with the body could be currently confronted. It is the present that contains the constant possibility of becoming unfamiliar with the own self.

Surely, the artistic frame of the research on using the negotiability of the body image for goals alternative to optimization and control enabled a very conscious research on what the bodies of the performers could potentially be and become. It is obvious that, due to the particular education as dancers, performers and/or choreographers, the members of the research team were especially qualified to play with the content of their individual body containers. Surely, most individuals outside the contemporary dance field have less awareness and knowledge of the different contents with which their bodies are confronted. At the same time it is obvious that the bodies outside the artistic field of choreography are equally filled with 'content' in our sense. However, with the difference that everyday processes of filling the body with content mostly happen on a less conscious, maybe even more subconscious level.

In contrast to the understanding of the body as an identity project, the notion of the body as a sensitive container does not equate the body with the own identity. By not equating the own body with the own identity, it might become easier to also integrate those aspects of the body which the neoliberal request for optimization and control must reject, namely the potentially volatile, fragile, or uncanny aspects of the body. This understanding of the body as a sensitive container that is potentially open to experimentation also shifts the focus to the body as a potential place where social norms and values can be negotiated, subverted, or changed. In this regard, the particular ways in which we use, name, and imagine our bodies are also political. Since both contemporary politics and contemporary economics are proving to be immensely interested in controlling how individuals use their bodies, the fact that the content of the body-container in its very nature is negotiable brings up questions of power. Shifting the focus away from working on the body's enhancement towards playing with the body's unfamiliar potential might also imply possibilities of re-creating and subverting dominant bodily images, modes of perception, as well as physical practices that are connected with the body.

Thinking further upon those lines, it seems relevant to find answers to the following questions: How can one enable a deeper awareness of those processes of filling the body with content on a social level? And where are the spaces and options that enable one to play with those alternative contents?

4.9 Sharing the first artistic research project with an audience

The structure of the graduate program "Performing Citizenship", during which the artistic research project "the bodies we are" took place, not only included the practical research process happening in the dance studio, but it also comprised a research presentation for an audience. But what could be an appropriate format to share the results of our research process?

This question led to a more fundamental question, namely: What is the difference between presenting the results of an artistic research process and the presentation of an artistic production process? As a contemporary choreographer, I would argue that also most of my artistic production processes include artistic research – in form of research on a particular phenomenon, movement, topic, relationship, structure, etc. However, this particular research must be rather goal-oriented since its particular purpose is feeding and supporting the production of a coherent choreographic work aimed at an audience.

In contrast to this, in my first artistic research project within the graduate program "Performing Citizenship", the purpose of the research was not to produce a coherent choreographic work, but to focus on the research itself.

This change of focus opened up a more notable freedom to investigate artistic strategies and methods, while not having to think about producing aesthetically interesting choreographic material for an audience. In this different context, however, the structural need for a "final" presentation in some ways was a bit tricky and even contradictory, since to some extent, it brought back some of the usual logic of aesthetic decisions that are part of every choreographic production process. At the same time, the task to present the results of the artistic research project seemed totally valid; why would I be funded to do an artistic research project and then not share this knowledge with an audience?[65]

The crucial question was, what kind of format to choose for sharing the research results: a lecture, or a lecture demonstration? However, at that time, those formats with their central focus on explanation via language felt inappropriate, since our research had mostly been based on physical experiments that needed to be experienced through the body. I could also have chosen the format of a practical workshop in the dance studio. But also this format felt inappropriate at that time, since I was not sure whether it would exclude people who were interested in the research yet who, due to their missing practical experience, would not take part in a practical workshop. Since this research presentation was hosted by K3 | Tanzplan Hamburg, which had a theater stage available, I finally chose the format of a staged performative setup. This decision however confronted me with the problem mentioned above; namely how to create a presentation structure for the stage, which would enable us to share our research results through an aesthetic experience, while at the same time making it clear that this was not an artistic production.[66]

Those questions also led to another issue, namely how to reprocess four weeks of practical research for a one-evening presentation? Reflecting the results of the artistic experiments in relation to the initial research question of how one could use the flexibility and openness of the body for goals other than self-optimization, I wanted the presentation to deal with several aspects. Firstly, I wanted the theater stage to become a place where the audience could

---

65 Surely this paper is also one way of sharing this research.
66 Regarding the question how the results of a particular artistic research process can be shared with an audience, also compare Sybille Peters' concept "show and tell". In this concept, Peters proposes the "performance-lecture" as a possible format situated between art and science. Cf. https://www.fundus-theater.de/wp-content/uploads/2017/09/brsch_showandtell.pdf (date accessed 5 January 2022)

follow different processes of creating and re-creating body images of the performers. And secondly, I wanted to create a frame concerning the discourse that would connect those processes to the social topic of the body as an identity project.

The presentation of the research and its choreographic structure

The spatial structure of the presentation of the research included a stage, a pink sofa and two large loudspeakers standing at both sides of it. It also included the use of different media, i.e., the physical movement of two performers, an audio of recorded sounds and language, and video-projected images and texts.

At the beginning of the presentation[67], the two[68] performers Vania Rovisco and Juli Reinartz were casually sitting on the pink sofa. While the audience was looking at them sitting, an audio file with a voice speaking was played from the loudspeakers.

> Antje, I have prepared a training for you... it is not just any training, it is a super training. It makes you super fit...and super open. It is the perfect embodiment training and the perfect coming-to-yourself-training. And the perfect opening-all-potentials-in-your-body-training. It is a training of your potential.

This audio clip was an excerpt of an experiment that I carried out with Juli Reinartz during our research period. Within this experiment on a verbal level we invented different kinds of "potential training" for each other by improvising with different quotes and clichés that we had appropriated from contemporary dance classes, yoga classes, but also wellness advertisements, etc.

With this combination of the casual presence of the performers' bodies not doing anything and the audio announcement of a fictitious "potential-training" I intended to create a first discursive frame, broaching the topic of self-enhancement and working on the own self. At the same time, with this initial scene, I intended to create questions in the audience, such as: What is the individual potential of those bodies we see sitting on the sofa? What could be the purpose of working on the own self?

---

67   For a video documentation also cf. https://vimeo.com/174128820
68   The co-researcher Johanna Roggan could not take part in the presentation because she was not available on the presentation dates.

4. The first artistic research project "The bodies we are" 117

After this first introductory scene, the light went off and the audience heard the sound of a windshield wiper, while a visual projection started. In this visual projection, I used images as well as language to visually and verbally communicate an experiment to the audience. In this regard, by announcing and explaining a performative experiment to the audience, the projection also functioned as another layer of a discursive frame.

1. image: ???
2. image: An experiment: Imagine that everyone of us possesses a multitude of possible bodies
3. image: NOW
4. image: Full-Beauty
5. image: LIZ
6. image: Kevin
7. image: strategies of body appropriation

By projecting this particular thought experiment, I intended to create a particular discursive claim: that any individual – including the audience – potentially has a multitude of possible body images available. In contrast to the belief in the own body as identity project with its demand of self-optimization, therefore primarily using the negotiability of the body to achieve a better version of the own self, the projected thought experiment proposed something very different. The three bodies projected as anyone's potential bodies hinted at a rather unusual and surprising connection to the neoliberal interest in working on one's own potential. By asserting that these three projected bodies could be anyone's potential bodies, I intended to create an irritation or questioning in the audience's mind: why should those other bodies be potential bodies of the own self?

In the next part of the presentation, the audience witnessed a process in which the performers played with different performative material that derived from the artistic research process. While in the research process we experimented with appropriating details from the depicted bodies we had collected to then, with the help of them, create different physical actions, perceptions. In the presentation, the performers considered this newly found physical and verbal material as choreographic material they performed for an audience. In order to make this process transparent for an audience, I structured it in such a way that I divided this process of recreating the performers' body images into four parts and again used visual projections to explain what the performers were focusing on.

1. Action – i.e. physical actions that we derived from each of the pictured bodies.
2. Shape – i.e. positions or postures that we derived from each of the pictured bodies.
3. Action & space of imagination – i.e. a combination of the assumed actions and verbally expressed needs and desires that derived from experiencing and performing those actions.
4. Action, shape & space of imagination. – a combination of all three layers.

Through this structural form, the audience was assisting a process in which the performers worked with some of the physical, sensory, and emotional material that was appropriated from each particular unfamiliar body from our artistic research. By alternating between performing different actions and shapes and also using language to express the particular desires and imaginations developed within the artistic research process, the performers consciously played with the creation of different body images within their own body containers.

As a conclusion, one can say that the chosen format of our research presentation aimed at sensitizing audience perception for the variety in outcome when creating and recreating the internal body image. At the same time, the audience had a chance to witness the actual process of construction by realizing how their own perception of a performer's body changed while they were following the different steps of the presentation. One can say that for the time of the research results being shown, the performers' bodies became the carriers of potential alternative body images that could be experienced from the inside as well as from the outside perspective. Due to the fact that those potential alternative body images would not be something the majority of people would normally identify with, the research presented also aimed at challenging the audience with an open question, i.e. what is the advantage of using the body for becoming unfamiliar with the own self? As one possible answer to this question the research presentation ended with a last visual projection, which was supposed to create a last discursive frame in the context of the performative actions the audience had just witnessed.

1. image: an appropriated body image could become a complex unfamiliar space of action.

2. image: potential: body images are possible spaces of action. You can influence your space of action any time.
3. image: You just appropriate a different body image.

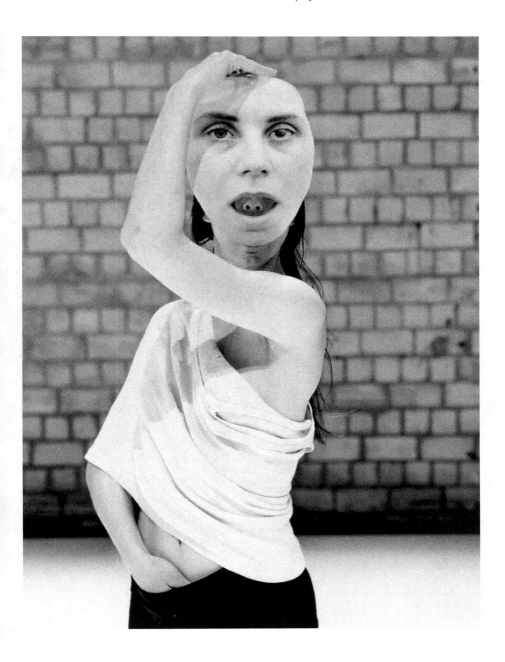

4. The first artistic research project "The bodies we are" 123

5. A historical perspective on the body and the ability to play with self-distancing

When researching on alternative perspectives on the body that do not primarily consider the body as a place and medium to work on the expression as well as the enhancement of the own self, a look into European history is also stimulating, since it reveals very diverse ideas of the body. In his book "The fall of public man"[1], the sociologist and historian Richard Sennett offers an interesting analysis of what a body was expected to be in the 18th, the 19th, and the 20th centuries. In this analysis, Sennett explains how and why the understanding of the body changed – from something impersonal to something personal – with the upcoming of the concept of individuality. What is particularly interesting in his analysis is that Sennett also describes the social effects of this change, at the same time proposing the thesis that the searching and longing for an individual self leads to an intimate society, as he calls it, i.e., a society suffering from narcissism and a loss of social interaction.

Based on Sennett's analysis in his book the "fall of public man", in this chapter, I will be dealing with the following questions: What alternatives to the concept of the body as identity project can be found when looking into European history? How and why did Western society arrive at the present notion of the body as an identity project and in what way has this thinking been affecting the social life within contemporary society? And, how might our knowledge about varying concepts of the body at different times in history inspire our imagination when dealing with today's concept and perception of the body as an identity project?

---

[1]   Sennett, Richard (1992) The Fall of Public Man

5.1 The body as something natural and impersonal in the Ancien Régime of the 18th century

If the understanding of the body as an expression of the own self has its origin in the 19th century, the question arises, how people perceived the body before that particular development. As can be assumed, Sennett's historical analysis shows that in the 18th century, when the concept of individuality did not yet exist, people had a very different idea of the body.

In order to comprehend the particular understanding of the body in the hierarchical feudal society of the 18th century, it is helpful to consider one of the basic principles that determined the social life in that period, a period that was marked by a radical distinction between private and public domain. In his analysis, Sennett points out that in the 18th century "man made himself in public, he realized his nature in the private realm, (...)."[2] Accordingly, people thought about public life as a highly artificial theater so that the people moving on this theater stage were considered to be actors. This concept of public life as theater went along with clear conventions: In 18th century feudal society, all public behavior was determined by conventional codes of expression such as gestures, use of language, or clothing, which affected all areas of public life.

The alternative to the public domain, ruled by conventional codes of expression, was the private domain of family life, which was the only place where the natural character of a person was allowed to come to life, if only to a certain extent. As already mentioned above, in the 18th century the notion of individuality did not yet exist, so what was considered to be a natural character of a person? Interestingly, natural character in the 18th century was not looked upon as something a single person was able to influence, but it was defined as the general character all human beings were assumed to have in common.[3] It thus becomes clear why the concept of individuality was simply not relevant in the thinking of the 18th century: people were either considered to be actors in a public world ruled by artificial conventions or people were "natural" characters like any other human being in a private domain.

This radical distinction between private and public domain also affected the particular understanding of the body in the 18th century. Consequently, the understanding of the body in private life was that it lived out general human drives, whereas the body in the public domain was not a product of individual

---

2   Sennett (1992), p. 18.
3   Cf. Sennett (1992), p. 152.

decisions but of obedience to social conventions. Therefore, all social classes had their particular physical appearances in public life, which were an indicator of their particular social standing.[4]

It is most likely that to a citizen of a democratic and individualized society of today the rigid social structure of the 18th century with its arbitrary codes of expression must feel rather strange und surely not desirable. However, what is interesting even from today's perspective is the fact that the combination of defining the body as something natural and at the same time impersonal, too, also created for the 18th century citizen a certain freedom in how they dealt with their own body.

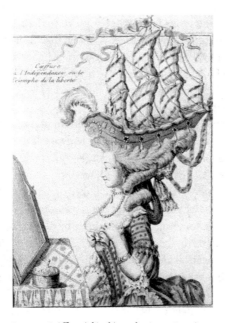

Image: Coiffure à l'indépendance ou Le triomphe de la liberté. Anonymous circa 1778. Found on: https://museefrancoamericain.fr/collection/objet/coiffure-de-lindependance-ou-le-triomphe-de-la-liberte (date accessed: 9 February 2022)

---

4   Cf. Sennett (1992), p. 65.

Because the outward appearance always depended on highly artificial and arbitrary codes of expression, people were able to self-distance themselves from their bodies and therefore did not regard them as something individual but rather as a kind of mannequin or, in other words, as an instrument or a toy with which to play.[5] Although the ability to self-distance themselves from their own bodies was a tool necessary to the citizens in all social classes, the biggest freedom in using the body as even a kind of playing toy could be found in the elite and wealthier bourgeoisie. According to Sennett, the upper class carried the principle of dressing the body as mannequin to its logical extreme; "by using the body as play toy they literally disembodied bodily imagery[6].

Taking the picture above as an example, one can see how this disembodiment of bodily imagery worked on a practical level. Accordingly, on first looking at the picture, one's gaze is most likely drawn to the enormous ship on the woman's head, an item which is used as an extension of the woman's body. From there, probably the gaze moves to the extraordinary headdress that looks like waves. Since both, the object and the headdress are so huge and exalted, they catch so much of the viewer's attention that the viewer's gaze hardly stays with the woman's face or body at all.

It is exactly this instance of being focused on an exalted object attached to a body, rather than being focused on the body itself that led Sennett to the conclusion that in the 18th century using the body as play toy in fact disembodied bodily imagery. Along the same lines, face paint, wigs, heads, or vest-coats were not used to underline the individual face or figure of a person, but the contrary was the case: the adornments attracted attention as objects in themselves, and therefore they objectified the body by distracting the viewer from the particular form of the body or the individual features of a person's face. This power of imagination and playfulness in the upper class clothing, that led to the disembodiment of bodily imagery, was applied by women and by men on equal terms.

Establishing a connection between the structure of 18th century society and the way individuals of different social classes were perceiving and using their bodies, one can come to the following conclusion: The existence of conventional codes of expression, accompanied by the belief that all people were actors, led to a social situation, in which the majority of citizens of that society were able to create a distance between their outward appearances and their

---

5   Cf. Sennett (1992), p. 64f.
6   Cf. Sennett (1992), p. 69.

own selves. The upper and therefore affluent class could even turn this distance between their outward appearances and their own selves into a remarkable ability to play with their own appearances in a sometimes most imaginative way.

5.2 The body as an expression of the inner self in the 19th century

From the 18th to the 19th century a cultural change took place, triggered by an evolving belief in secularism as well as by the economics of industrial capitalism. According to Sennett, this cultural change had a radical effect on public life, among other things, it led to the entering of individual personality into the public domain – which, in turn also affected how people perceived and used their bodies. Regarding the evolving belief in secularism, Sennett states:

> "Things and people were understandable in the 18th Century when they could be assigned a place in the order of Nature. (...) The secularism which arose in the 19th Century was of a wholly antithetical sort. It was based on a code of the immanent, rather than the transcendent. Immediate sensation, immediate fact, immediate feeling, were no longer to be fitted into a pre-existent scheme in order to be understood. The immanent, the instant, the fact, was a reality in and of itself."[7]

It is not surprising that, as a consequence, this new secular world view also impacted on people's perception of physical bodies. While in the 18th century people did not consider the body to be something individual, in the 19th century, people started to believe that all details of the body had a particular immanent meaning and that those details in turn revealed physical as well as psychological aspects of a person's character. Since the immanent meaning varied from person to person, the physical as well as the psychological character of a person was believed to vary, too. Therefore, Sennett points out that this was the moment when the belief in personality entered the public domain, because "these immediate impressions different people produced were taken to be their personalities."[8]

---

7   Sennett (1992), p. 21.
8   Sennett (1992), p. 152.

The new secular worldview that all things and people could actually be defined by their appearance, also produced radical changes in the internal perception of the own self. If one is what one appears, every change in the outward appearance, every subtle change in the way of expressing emotion, in clothing, or gestures was read and understood as a change in that person's own particular self. The belief that all appearances have personal meanings went along with a second belief, namely that appearance and impulse can be interpreted as one and the same – which meant that people took a particular appearance for a direct expression of the "inner" self.[9],[10]

Combined with one another, these two beliefs produced a tremendous fear of involuntarily and seemingly disclosing one's own feelings, a fear that was especially strong in women. Since there always seemed to be the risk that the body would reveal some immoral feelings or desires of the particular person, the body became a potential risk: people could not control how their particular body was read, i.e., there was the fear that the body would appear to express the individual character beyond the control of the individual him- or herself. However, controlling one's expression was not possible through action, but only through being vigilant towards oneself and a constant attempt at defining and controlling one's own feelings.[11]

This in turn forced people to focus on their individual internal world of feelings and perceptions, while it simultaneously strictly reduced their physical expressions in public. The fear of being perceived as 'wrong' or 'immoral' led to a general withdrawal of women and men into the private domain of the family. Since people had no strategies to create a distance between their appearances and their own selves, they were forced to take their physical as well as emotional expressions for their individual personalities. At the same time, they constantly doubted their own personalities so that, consequently, this led to questions such as "How do I appear to others? What do I myself feel? Who am I? Is this really me?, etc."

One can conclude that the fact of immediate appearance being accepted as a guide to inner feeling was the basic pre-condition for the belief in individ-

---

9 Cf. Sennett (1992), p. 153.
10 These two beliefs can be found in the 19th century flourishing practice of phrenology – the reading of character from the physical shape of the head. Compare for example: Wells, Samuel Roberts: How to Read Character: a New Illustrated Handbook of Phrenology and Physiognomy, for Students and Examiners.
11 Cf. Sennett (1992), p. 152.

ual personality to develop. However, according to Sennett, it is also the economics of industrial capitalism that had an impact on this development. The economics of industrial capitalism of the 19th century fostered the entering of the concept of personality into public life. Why was that so?

With the evolution of industrial capitalism the production system changed from hand-made to machine-made goods that could be produced more quickly and in much larger numbers. The vast increase in produced goods in turn required that people would buy more. Yet, first of all, people needed to actually be motivated to increase their level of consumption. The question was how that could be achieved, how, for example, a woman could be induced to buy five machine-made dresses, when, before, two hand-made dresses had been sufficient?

In order to make people buy a larger amount of mostly nondescript goods, it was not sufficient to just offer the objects. In order to reach a higher level of consumption, retailers invented a new selling strategy: they endowed their products, by association and mystification, with an interest the merchandise on its own might intrinsically lack.[12] By showing an image of the product in an exotic landscape or by presenting a famous person wearing a particular article of clothing, retailers connected a particular product with particular desires of the consumers. As a consequence of this mystification of goods, achieved with the help of advertising strategies, consumption of per se uniform and mass-produced goods began to be accepted as an expression of individual personality.

Considering all those different developments together, one can draw the following conclusions concerning the understanding of the body in the 19th century. Because of the belief that all appearances have personal meaning and express the "inner" self, the individual body became a means of firstly expressing one's own individual personality, and secondly, a means of reading and decoding other persons' individual personalities. Simultaneously, the body became a risk, a possible traitor: if every detail could be a possible hint to one's own personality, the expression of the body was hardly controllable. The marketing strategies of industrial capitalism perfectly solved this social and psychological dilemma: by artificially connecting nondescript, mass-produced goods with individual desires and interests, the act of consuming products made it possible to combine two contradictory desires, namely blending into

---

12   Cf. Sennett (1992), p. 144.

the crowd and not attracting unwanted attention on the one hand, and being an individual with a particular personality and expression on the other hand.

5.3 The non-social but intimate body in the 20th and early 21st century

According to Sennett, the development of the belief in individual personality with its constant search for selfhood, went on in the course of the 20th century and led to an intimate society characterized by a high level of narcissism.[13] As part of his analysis, Sennett claims that within the course of the 20th century the belief in individual personality including the constant search for selfhood becomes highly problematic, since it finally leads to a destruction of social interaction within public life. The reason for this problematic development Sennett attributes to the loss of self-distance, which he considers to be an outcome of the belief in individual personality.

Yet, in the morally liberal Western society of the 20th and early 21st century, the loss of self-distancing has become particularly problematic – and for what reason? The answer to this question begins to evolve when connecting Sennett's analysis with Gugutzer's thesis about the 1970s and 1980s process of individualization with its shift from values such as duty and obedience to values such as autonomy and self-fulfillment. In the course of this shift, the individual gained a higher level of agency and more freedom to take his or her own decisions, while simultaneously the role of the body became increasingly important. Since the own body was and is what is always available to the individual, the body became the perfect place in which to live and perform this newly gained agency. While in the 19th century the body was perceived as something hardly controllable, in the course of the 20th century the understanding of the body changed and it was considered to be something that can be actively formed in a self-determined way. Or as Gugutzer put it: In the 1970s and 1980s process of individualization the body became an identity project that the individual could always hold onto. Because of its permanent availability, visible and perceivable effects could be produced with the help of and via the body, and certainty and identity, too.[14]

---

13 Cf. Sennett (1992), p. 220.
14 Cf. Gugutzer (2015), p. 43.

What became problematic in the course of the 20th and early 21st century with regard to that loss of self-distancing can be called the flip side of this newly gained agency, namely the fact that the less restricted the individual is through duty and obedience, the more responsible he or she becomes for his or her own decisions. As long as the own decisions lead to success, including a mainstream appearance and socially favored perceptions and feelings, this might not be a problem. However, the problem starts where the result of the own decisions is failure, that is to say if, as a result of one's own decisions, the own appearance, feelings or perceptions differ from the mainstream.

In this case, the neoliberal imperative of self-fulfillment and self-optimization of the 20th and early 21st century, intertwined with the understanding of the body as an identity project, becomes problematic, since there is absolutely no escape from the postulate of being the own self. Therefore, in the 20th and early 21st century, being oneself and using the body as an identity project becomes a rather serious undertaking that had better not fail. Taking this into account and connecting it with the initial question of how to emancipate the body from the neoliberal imperative of optimization and control, one will realize that this undertaking is quite a challenge. In a society in which individuals have no or only very limited strategies for self-distancing from the own body and self, escaping from the socially accepted norms and imperatives becomes a real challenge.

According to Sennett, the loss of self-distancing in the 20th century not only has an impact on the personal, private life but also has a radical effect on the social interaction within the society.[15] In the 18th century social codes of expression built an impersonal social terrain that could be used for social exchange. Within this social terrain, even people that were not perceived as equal were able to meet and interact by using impersonal codes of expression. Yet, the later belief in individual personality that went along with rejecting impersonal forms of expression, has taken away this common ground and has led to the circumstance that the stranger himself becomes a threatening figure[16]. Consequently, according to Sennett, it becomes a desirable state to feel closeness, while its contraries such as foreignness, alienation, and impersonality become avoided states.[17]

---

15 Cf. Sennett (1992), p. 261.
16 Cf. Sennett (1992), p. 3.
17 Cf. Sennett (1992), p. 259.

Since people cannot distance themselves from their own selves and since there are no impersonal forms of expression that can be used as common terrain, within the European culture of the 20th and early 21st century, the meeting of people and things that are different from their own selves must lead to attributions of "otherness". These attributions of "otherness" then lead to alienation and separation from one another, which in turn makes identification with different people, backgrounds, or cultures practically impossible.

In his analysis Sennett hints at one important social consequence of this development. What gets lost in the intimate society's longing for closeness, is the idea that one grows only by processes of encountering the unknown. He states:

> "Things and persons which are strange may upset familiar ideas and received truths; unfamiliar terrain serves a positive function in the life of human beings. The function it serves is to accustom the human being to take risks. Love of the ghetto, especially the middle-class ghetto, denies the person a chance to enrich his perceptions, his experience, and learn that most valuable of all human lessons, the ability to call the established conditions of life into question."[18]

But what exactly is that kind of ability that is needed to call the established conditions of life into question, which also seems to be relevant when emancipating oneself from the actual social imperative of self-optimization? According to Sennett, it is an ability that gets lost the minute self-distancing gets lost: it is the ability to play. While in the 18th century with its tradition of theatrum mundi, by having to deal with external rules and conventions, all members of society were engaged in practices of play, in the intimate society, the ability to practice playing, while simultaneously accepting the risk of failure, is mostly reduced to the social life of children or to artistic practice. In his analysis Sennett argues that it is precisely that practice of playing that prepares children for the experience of playacting and self-distancing. Since every play is based on particular external and impersonal rules, it teaches children to treat external conventions of behavior as believable.[19]

Following those external rules leads to self-distancing since those rules are not connected to immediate desires of the self. Sennett states: "When children

---

18   Sennett (1992), p. 295.
19   Cf. Sennett (1992), p. 266.

have learned to believe in conventions, then they are ready to do qualitative work on expression by exploring, changing, and redefining the quality of these conventions."[20]

Following this thesis, one can conclude that the process of learning to follow external rules and conventions in play does not lead to mere obedience and consequently the loss of agency of the subject, but to the contrary, namely the ability to negotiate and even change the external rules if necessary.

Relating all of this to the body, it follows that the more the body becomes a place where individual personality is supposed to be expressed, the more difficult it becomes to implement any form of negotiation or change regarding one's own body image. Because of the particular social circumstances we are bound to, as citizens of a neoliberal society with its strong imperatives of self-enhancement, most individuals are trained to regard their physical bodies as a result of individual self-expression and precisely not as a result of playacting, which then succumbs to external conventions and rules. This difficulty to think of the body as a tool to play with non-personal forms of expression, not only impedes self-distancing but also makes it difficult to distance oneself from any social demand with regard to the body, such as optimization or control.

In my particular research process, Sennett's analysis created an interest in the following questions: What could, today, be a contemporary way of playing with impersonal forms of expression applied to the own body? In which social situations could individuals benefit from using the body not as a place to express the own identity, but to play with impersonal forms of expression? How could the artistic field be used to develop different performative practices to play with the creation of manifold temporal identities?

---

20 Sennett (1992), p. 266.

6. The second artistic research project "Let's face it!"

When planning the second research project, my interest in researching on strategies that could be used to play with self-distancing met with another topic that was very present in the media at that time, namely the increasing use of facial recognition software in public areas. The technical development of facial recognition apps in 2016, such as "FindFace", made it technically possible to photograph individuals in public space and identify the person with 70% reliability.[1] This newly developed facial recognition technique opened up a discussion about surveillance and the right of anonymity in public space.[2] How could individuals protect themselves from this new form of surveillance? Following this debate, I became interested in the human face as a particular body part that is central for identifying an individual. How could the choreographic field be used to develop strategies that could be used to distance oneself from the own individual face in order to blur the own identity?

Thus, in my second research project "Let's face it!" I examined the appropriation of three fictitious body images; a body without a face, a face without a body and a body with plenty of faces. This research also led to a deeper interest in the topic of the mask. In the context of my research, I considered the mask as a means for simultaneously hiding and showing oneself, a medium that can be used to playfully transform into another being and temporarily disappear as an identifiable subject.[3]

---

1   Cf. https://www.theguardian.com/technology/2016/may/17/findface-face-recognitio n-app-end-public-anonymity-vkontakte (date accessed 5 January 2022)
2   Cf. https://www.forbes.com/sites/thomasbrewster/2020/01/29/findface-rolls-out-hu ge-facial-recognition-surveillance-in-moscow-russia/ (date accessed 5 January 2022)
3   Cf. Brauneck (2020), p. 9.

6.1 Preparing the artistic research

To prepare for my second research project "Let's face it!", I invited the performer and choreographer Vania Rovisco and the visual artist Sophie Aigner. Both of them had already taken part in the first research project "the bodies we are". This second research took place from December 2016 to January 2017 at the studios of K3 | Tanzplan Hamburg, Kampnagel Hamburg, and of Tanzfaktur Cologne. In order to realize this research project, I also applied for additional funding. Since the funding was granted as project funding, it also had an impact on the actual process of the research, i.e. this research had to result in a stage performance piece.[4] Because of this formal requirement, I divided the research into two phases. In the first phase we invented and acted out various experiments that had been derived from the questions I have shared above, while in the second phase, the results of those experiments were used as choreographic material.

Before starting the practical research period with Vania Rovisco and Sophie Aigner in the studio, I did some preliminary research on artistic works and also on texts focusing on the face and the use of different strategies for blurring or subverting individual identity. I compiled this "archive of interests"[5] with artistic works such as the "History portraits" by Cindy Sherman[6], "three studies of the human head" by Francis Bacon[7], the project "URME" by Leonardo Sel-

---

[4] The decision to apply for artistic project funding, was mainly influenced by financial issues. In the frame of the graduate program the financial support for the individual research projects was limited to 2000 Euros. In order to provide for an appropriate payment for the external research-team, I decided to apply for additional funding. At that time, there were hardly any funding possibilities for artistic research projects in Germany, (and still there are very few). Thus, I decided to connect the research to the creation of a choreographic work, which then allowed me to apply for project funding. I am aware that in terms of research, in some regards this is also problematic and my decision was also critically discussed within the graduate program, since project funding also brings about the need to think within the demands of artistic production, which in some ways is different from the concerns of the research.

[5] The materials of this archive were chosen intuitively. They were materials I personally found interesting because of aesthetic or conceptual reasons.

[6] Cf. Schneider, Christa (2012) Cindy Sherman. History Portraits.

[7] https://www.francis-bacon.com/artworks/paintings/three-studies-human-head (date accessed 5 January 2022)

vaggio[8], the work of the photographer Ralph Eugene Meatyard[9], the film "Persona"[10] by Ingmar Bergman or a poetic text on the face by Rainer Maria Rilke[11]. Additionally, it also included theoretical text material such as "Year Zero: Faciality" by Gilles Deleuze and Félix Guattari[12], and also a compilation of various texts on the use of masks in different societies by Hans Belting.

When looking at the collected material, my aim was to extract from it concrete practices concerning the face that other artists had worked with and in which they had used the face to achieve a destabilization of identity within their particular artistic medium. The strategies and practices I found in the collected material were: layering and merging faces, cutting faces out and then pasting them, multiplying faces, giving faces away, using the face as protective shield, blurring and smudging faces, using abstract and foreign or even alien faces in the form of masks, or inserting alien elements into a face.

I looked into the theoretical texts I had collected[13] with a different aim in mind. I was interested in using them as an archive of alternative concepts of the face, which would then challenge my own imagination during my own process of artistic research. The ideas I collected were: the concept of only having a limited number of faces available[14], the necessity of giving a rest to the own face in order not to abrade it, the concept of the face as a white wall/black hole system that produces variations of faces according to what the changeable combinations of its cogwheels have been set to[15], the concept of impersonal faces in the form of masks, the use of masks as a tool for transformation and also transportation[16].

---

8   http://www.urmesurveillance.com/ (date accessed 5 January 2022)
9   Cf. Parry, Eugenia; Siegel, Elizabeth (eds.) (2011) Ralph Eugene Meatyard. Dolls and Masks.
10 Bergman, Ingmar (1966) Persona. Film.
11 Cf. Schmidt Bergmann, Hansgeorg (ed.) (2000) Rainer Maria Rilke: Die Aufzeichnungen des Malte Laurids Brigge, p. 11f.
12 Cf. Deleuze, Gilles; Guattari, Félix (1988) Year Zero: Faciality. In: A thousand plateaus: capitalism and schizophrenia. p. 167–191.
13 The materials of this archive were chosen on the basis of an intuitive interest. They were materials I personally found inspiring when developing alternative ways of thinking about the human face.
14 I appropriated this idea of borrowing a face from someone else from a poetic text of Rainer Maria Rilke. Cf. Schmidt Bergmann (ed.) (2000), p. 11f.
15 This idea was derived from Deleuze's and Guattari's thoughts on the face. Cf. Deleuze, Gilles; Guattari, Félix (1988), p. 168.
16 Cf. Belting (2014), p. 50f.

In comparison to the first research project "the bodies we are", in which the research itself took place within the field of choreography, "Let's face it!" was designed as an interdisciplinary research-project between the choreographic field and the field of visual art. My particular approach to it was that I shared exactly the same research question for every artistic field, yet the working material and methods of those two separate fields remained different. Accordingly, in the process of preparation, I met the visual artist Sophie Aigner, in order to share my research questions with her and exchange about her approach to these questions.

Coming from the field of visual arts, Aigner was very interested in what kind of clothing and objects people use to partly or even completely disappear as individual subjects, such as: hazes, masks, sunglasses, camouflage clothing, fur, and false hair. Concerning the question of how a face without a body or, alternatively, a body without a face could be created, Aigner had the spontaneous association of wooden boards that leave a cutout hole for the face, the kind of one can find in tourist areas, amusement parks, or at private festivities. Aigner's proposal was a very easy and playful solution for the question of how to separate the face from the body. With the wooden boards, it would become possible to either see the face, but hide the body – or, alternatively, to see the body without seeing the face. Together we decided that this idea of a plain surface with a cutout hole for the face would be a spatial setup we would both like to work with during the practical research.

The second decision on the material to be used, was also taken during this preparatory meeting and it developed from a fascination with the strategy of layering faces, which was inspired by Bergman's film "PERSONA". Bergman in his medium of film achieved the layering of faces by actually placing two different images on top of each other with the help of film technology. So we started to think about how to appropriate this strategy for the different types of medium we would be using. Aigner proposed approaching the strategy of layering faces by first connecting it with the activity of multiplying them. Therefore Aigner suggested using various types of medium, such as photography and drawing, but also molding the face with latex and plaster, in order to create multiple imprints of the performer's particular face. This method would technically allow us to detach the face from the body and also to create a variety of one- and two-dimensional faces that could then be layered. This practical interest then led to the artistic practice of creating different masks made of latex, plaster and paper, alternatively.

6. The second artistic research project "Let's face it!"   141

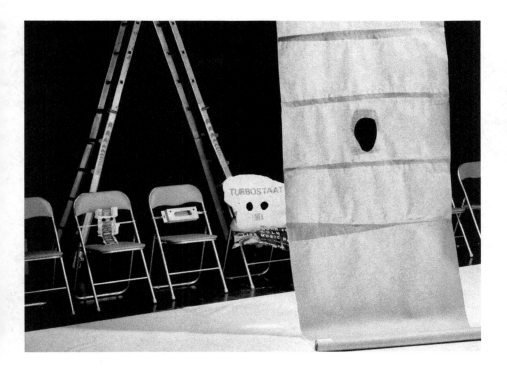

6.2 Artistic experiments: On a face without a body

Below I will reflect on the artistic research experiments concerning a face without a body, in which we used plain sheets of paper with cutouts[17] to separate the face from the body. Starting out from the assumption, that in the European culture, the face is predominantly used as a place to identify the individual with[18], I defined the central interest when artistically experimenting with the face without a body as the developing of alternative potentials of using the face. Accordingly, the research started with a very basic question, namely: The face on its own, what can it do?[19]

> Experiment "actions of the face"
> Sit comfortably on a chair and direct all your attention to your face. Investigate different activities you can do with your face only. As a second step use the found results in order to create short movement sequences with the face.

In this particular experiment, my interest was to research the performer's internal subjective perception of the own face. Thus, the experiment invited the performer to explore different potential movements and micro-movements in the face, involving the tension and release of different muscle groups in the face as well as possible movements in jaw and eyes. Reflecting on the experiences of the performers, one can state that the potential actions of the face could be divided into three different areas. Firstly, into the area of facial expressions, the face can indicate feelings and impulses (such as joy, fear, anger, etc.). Secondly, with the help of its sensory organs, the face reflects the process of sensory perception (such as seeing, smelling, tasting, hearing). And thirdly, the face contains several openings that on a functional level can be opened and closed due to muscular and joint structures. Through these openings (such as eyes, mouth, ears, nostrils), the face can also excrete different fluids (e.g. tears, spittle, and snot).

---

17   Also cf. photos on p. 141f.
18   Cf. Belting (2014), p. 10.
19   This interest in the face as a medium for communication and expression is also central in other choreographic works, such as Antonia Baehr's choreography "For faces" or Jule Flierl's choreography "dissociation study".

The interesting insight developed during this experiment was, how easily the subjective internal perception of what the own face is and does can actually be transformed. A particular facial expression, for example a smile, could be perceived as an expression of internal feeling, but after shifting the focus for example to the muscular level, the same smile could also be perceived as just pure physical movement, without any emotional content. Interestingly, the longer the experiment went on, the easier it became for the performers to playfully shift between different functions and, alternatively, internal perceptions related to the face. Accordingly, when reflecting on the individual experience, the performer stated that, during the course of the experiment, the own face was not primarily perceived as a place of personal expression, but as a body part with lots of different functions, such as a "gate" between inside and outside of the body, or a "wet space" that absorbs external objects and assimilates them, or as a camera that records the external space, etc. Based on these insights of how to alternate between various internal perceptions of the face, I created another experiment, in which I put the focus on researching on non-personal facial expressions by following the idea of "borrowing faces" from someone else.

Experiment "Facial expression roulette"
Take five portrait photos of different persons with different facial expressions. Imitate these facial expressions with as many details as you can until you know them well. Stand behind a paper wall with a hole that just shows your face and zip through the five images plus add one relaxed face. Create a simple rhythm in your mind that you can play along with while moving from one face to the other.

The aim of this experiment was to explore the correlation between a particular facial expression and the corresponding emotional feeling generally ascribed as a norm to this facial expression within the social context.[20] At the

---

20   This interest in the relationship between a particular posture, tension, or way of moving and a corresponding emotional state, was also researched by the Russian director Vsevolod Meyerhold, who developed Biomechanics in the 1920s, which is a system of actor training. In Biomechanics, Meyerhold, a former student of Stanislawsky, was interested in the question how a conscious use of the physical body can raise particular emotions in the actor when performing a role. Biomechanics inverted the notion that the actors' movements and postures were "automatic" consequences of the inner experience, and instead asserted that the actors' physiology determined the consti-

beginning of the experiment, from Rovisco's internal perception, every particular facial expression such as smiling or looking annoyed and so on, simultaneously produced a particular physical and emotional echo in her body in the form of a physical tension or a feeling. Taking the knowledge of the cognitive development of children into account, one can assume that this connection between facial expression and internal emotion is part of our cultural 'vocabulary', since from early childhood on human beings learn to connect particular facial expressions with particular emotional states.[21] Once learnt, a particular facial expression such as anger, for example, will produce a correlating emotional feeling in the body, which also implies a particular muscular tension, etc.

However, in the course of the experiment, an interesting change took place in Rovisco's internal perception of her face. While repeating and rhythmically playing with the different facial expressions, from the internal perception, the performer felt that the more playfully she zipped through the chosen facial expressions, the more the initial emotional echo in the body decreased until it finally vanished altogether. One could conclude that through the action of playfully zipping through different facial expressions, the chosen facial expressions transformed into rather functional movement and were no longer attached to any expressive meaning. Because of this new disconnection between facial expressions and internal feelings, the performer's face started to feel to her like something unfamiliar that, similar to a mask, had artificially been put on the head as though it were a moving surface.

The experiment evoked changes in Rovisco's perception as a performer, but it evoked changes in my perception as an observer, too. In my role as a spectator, in the beginning of the experiment, I still tried to read the facial expressions according to the socially learnt meanings. However, in the course of the experiment, the socially learnt ability to decode the meaning of facial expressions got seriously impeded by firstly the high frequency of changes and secondly the fact that Rovisco's body was not visible. Since the body was not visible, there was no visible body or individual I could connect the emotional ex-

---

tution of the enacted role. Cf. also: Law, Alma H.; Gordon, Mel (2012) Meyerhold, Eisenstein and Biomechanics. Actor training in Revolutionary Russia.

21 Cf. Wellman, H.M; Harris, P. L ; Banerjee, M. ; Sinclair, A. (1995) Early understanding of emotion: evidence from natural language. Cognition and Emotion, 9(2/3), p. 117–149. Cf. Denham, S. A. (1986) Social Cognition, Prosocial Behavior, and Emotion in Preschoolers: Contextual Validation. Child Development, 57(1), p. 194–201.

pression to – so that consequently, after a while, I perceived Rovisco's face as something disembodied, artificial, and machine-like.

One can conclude that in the context of the artistic experiment, the moment a facial expression could not be traced back to a corresponding emotional source located in the body, the face, in the internal as well as the external perception, very easily got perceived as something artificial, machine-like, or even non-human. This is why in the internal perception of the performer, the experiments concerning a "face without a body" produced a particular form of self-distancing. This self-distancing could be understood as a state in which the performer perceived her individual facial expressions not as expressions associated with her internal emotions, but as pure physicality, pure movement. Since Rovisco's way of perceiving and also using her individual face as something rather machine-like was so fundamentally different from how the individual face is generally perceived and used in the social context, namely as a mirror of the individual's feelings and intentions, the experiment produced a state of disorientation in me as an observer. This disorientation could be described as an insecurity that derived from the difficulty of decoding Rovisco's facial expressions.

Assuming that the disorientation that was produced in me as a spectator resulted from Rovisco's unfamiliar use of her face, several questions came up: Did the irritation of the socially learnt understanding of the individual face produce an uncanny feeling one would rather avoid? Or could this state of disorientation also be perceived as an invitation to become aware of alternative potentials of the face? In other words: How could one invent alternative forms of faces, by playfully using the face's surface and forms, its openings, its holes, or its exceeding liquids in different ways? How could one invent faces that become an entity of their own, a kind of body in themselves whose functions could be re-invented? The aim of those questions was to create alternative, maybe not yet known imaginations and perceptions of the individual face, to irritate or surprise the individual knowledge of the face.

Experiment: "bodily functions in the face"
Select three of your bodily functions (what your body does) and transfer them to particular elements in your face. For example: Walk with your right eye, embrace things and people with your left eye. Digest through your mouth.

Experiment: "face as surveillance camera"
Close your right eye – so that your perception changes from 3D to 2D. Choose one point in space where you stand or sit. Your neck can only do horizontal or vertical movements. Imagine that your left eye is recording everything it sees.

Experiment: "face as string-instrument"
Experiment with using your face as a string instrument. Materials available: printed eye on cardboard, elastic strap fixed to the cardboard eye, blue balloon, blue surface.

The experiments described above were developed as answers to the questions raised above. In Rovisco's perception as a performer, the experiments allowed her to further develop her perception of the own face as something alien, something that she could not clearly label. At the same time, Rovisco perceived the experiments as an invitation to immerse in a different state of being, which she personally felt highly enjoyable. Rovisco's process of inventing alternative functions in the face and perceiving and using her individual face as an instrument or as a surveillance camera produced very different kinds of faces that Rovisco described as bodies in their own rights.

From the outside perspective of witnessing the experiments, all of those "bodies" were rather strange bodies: leaking holes, machine-like technical beings, or strange musical instruments. As a spectator, I was confronted with a variety of unusual associations regarding Rovisco's face. In the beginning of the experiment, my associations were mostly connected to the area of mental disease. Also, associations of ugliness, strangeness, and alienation were very acute. In my perception, witnessing the experiment produced rather unpleasant and partly even embarrassing feelings in me. Since the particular way in which Rovisco was using her facial functions was so different from the known use, I, as an observer, obviously had no strategies of decoding the facial expressions. Interestingly, my feeling of distance changed during the course of the experiment. This change happened when I, as an observer, could let go of my first associations and made the decision to encounter the performer's body and face with a different, more analytical as well as curious gaze. This particular gaze made it possible for me to encounter the newly created faces by focusing on their textures, rhythms and surfaces, by searching for their surprising elements, intentions, and humor without the need to immediately label my own perceptions.

What conclusion can be drawn from all the experiments concerning the face without a body? Although, due to our cultural imprint, individual faces are usually perceived as an expression and proof of the individual self, the experiments showed that this understanding can be questioned by playing with the different functions of the face. This playing around enabled Rovisco to create and perceive faces outside the range of what she would usually consider her individual face[22], such as her face as a surface with leaking wholes, as a machine like being, or as a string instrument. In this regard, the artistic experiments allowed Rovisco to use her face not only as a communication tool and representative of the own self, but as a playground in which she could rehearse other temporal versions of her face.

6.3 Theoretical perspective: Play as a process taking place "in between"

In his book "Truth and method"[23], Gadamer reflects on the artistic field as a playing field in which subjects become able to temporarily step out of the seriousness of purposes that determine their existence in their everyday reality. According to Gadamer, play has a special, ambivalent relation to what is serious.[24] On the one hand, the player knows that play is only play and that it exists in a world determined by the seriousness of purposes. At the same time, play contains its own seriousness, since playing only fulfills its purpose if the player is willing to fully engage in the process of playing. Play, in Gadamer's sense, is considered to be a back and forth movement, without a preset goal or purpose, which rather renews itself through constant repetition. It is also an integral part of play that it happens without strain.[25]

In contrast to Schiller, who defines play as an inner-subjective capacity of playing with the individual cognitive power[26], Gadamer states that play has its own essence, independent of those who play. Accordingly, he does not consider the players as subjects of play, but rather as individuals experiencing play

---

22 In the artistic research process, we did not investigate the usual individual perceptions of the face.
23 Gadamer, Hans-Georg (2004) Truth and Method
24 Cf. Gadamer (2004), p. 102.
25 Cf. Gadamer (2004), p. 104.
26 Also cf. p. 97f. of this paper.

by being engaged in it. In this perspective, play is understood as something that absorbs the player. However, play is no rigid system that predetermines the actions of the players. It is a "playing field"[27], a closed world, in which individuals experience the freedom of making individual decisions for one or the other possibility. As Gadamer states, this freedom of decision making in the playing field also bears a risk.[28] Since one can play only with serious possibilities, a particular individual decision might lead to a situation in which the player becomes so immersed in play that he or she becomes dominated by it. Therefore, Gadamer states that play is not only something the individual does, but play is actually something that has the power to master the players. In this sense, all playing is actually being played, since the individual is affected by the experiences created during the play.[29]

For Gadamer, it also seems characteristic for human play that it plays something.[30] By wanting to play, the individual separates the own behavior from its other behavior and, in doing that, chooses particular possibilities. Gadamer describes these choices as playful tasks the individual sets him- or herself. The purpose of play is the performance and experience of a task that implies a process of ordering and shaping the movement of the play itself. Since those tasks are not connected to an achievement of predefined goals, the only function and purpose of play is its own realization, i.e., its own self-presentation.[31]

In the context of art, the presentation of a playing process exceeds the closed playing field of an individual player. In the field of art, Gadamer states, the playing field opens toward a spectator. Therefore he defines playing in the field of art as a process that takes place "in between"[32], since the experiences of the player meet with an audience that, in turn, perceives the process of playing from an external perspective. Since artistic presentation always exists for an audience (even if this audience is absent), it is the spectator for and in whom the play is played. Because the spectator is the one to whom the play is presented, the spectator becomes involved in the play through his own experiences and thoughts that are created by the play.

---

27   Cf. Gadamer (2004), p. 107.
28   Cf. Gadamer (2004), p. 106.
29   Cf. Gadamer (2004), p. 106.
30   Cf. Gadamer (2004), p. 107.
31   Cf. Gadamer (2004), p. 108.
32   Cf. Gadamer (2004), p. 108.

Relating Gadamer's thesis that playing happens "in between" the artist and the spectator to our artistic experiments on a face without a body, one can also consider my individual experiences as an observer as part of the playing process. As described above, in the beginning of the experiments, my particular role in this playing process was rather passive, since I was mostly occupied with my own irritation and my rather unpleasant feelings resulting from it. Interestingly, this role changed during the course of the experiments. My difficulty of applying known strategies of reading the performer's face and the irritation that resulted from it forced me to actively search for alternative ways of reading Rovisco's face. My conscious decision to change my own gaze to a more curious and analytical perception could also be described as actively stepping into the present playing process. Becoming part of the playing process in turn allowed me as an observer to experience Rovisco's face in yet unknown ways, which expanded my understanding of the potentials of a human face.

6.4 Artistic experiments: On a body with plenty of faces & bodies without faces

In the following chapter I will change my focus and put it on a body that has access to a multitude of faces, which can count as yet another approach to experimenting with the face as a place on which to create and perform self-distancing. Due to this focus, the experiments were based on the artistic and conceptual proposition that a face is something one can playfully put on and take off, one can give away, one can borrow from someone, one can create of several layers, that can merge with others or that can be cut out and pasted onto a base. This proposition suited and was supported by Sophie Aigner's artistic interest in multiplying faces by producing different imprints and using those imprints to produce several masks from diverse materials, such as latex, paper, hard plaster, or cardboard. Accordingly, in the experiments concerning a body with plenty of faces, masks were used as a central tool. In the particular context of my artistic research process, I considered the mask as a means for simultaneously hiding and showing oneself, a medium that can be used to playfully transform into another being and temporarily disappear as an identifiable subject.[33] This understanding of the mask radically differs from the use of masks in the present Corona crisis, where wearing masks in most cases is

---

33 Cf. Brauneck (2020), p. 9.

6. The second artistic research project "Let's face it!" 151

not related to taking pleasure in any kinds of transformations, but rather to a pragmatic fear of being infected with the COVID-19 virus.

When researching on the mask as a tool with which to produce self-distancing, it was also rewarding to learn how differently masks are used in miscellaneous cultural contexts. In many African, Asian, and American cultures and cultural practices, masks have been and still are used as a tool for transformation that will allow the carrier to become someone or something else.[34] In these cultural contexts, masks are used, for example, as a communication tool with gods, ancestors or other species, or as a tool to travel to places that would otherwise not be accessible[35]. Yet in the last 1000 years of European culture, as Hans Belting points out, the mask has never been considered to be a tool for spiritual and perceptual transformation; rather it was looked upon as something that fulfills the function of hiding the "real" identity of an individual.[36] In this sense, in the European culture, masks were and still are used by individuals rather as a tool for acting and behaving outside his or her usual character without them being recognized, like in political demonstrations or in the carnival tradition, for example.

Even though I was aware of the scope of potential of the masks that can be found in different cultural contexts, in the artistic research process, I consciously did not decide beforehand on any particular function of the masks. This is why the masks Aigner created within the artistic research process did not have a particular prescribed use or function, but Aigner built them intuitively following her interest in materiality and form. Nevertheless, each mask had very distinctive features. However, these distinctive features were not the result of a prescribed narrative, but of its particular shape and the particular material from which it had been made.

In the experiments on bodies with plenty of faces, I investigated the following questions: Using the masks as tools, what kind of performative practices can be developed to create self-distancing? How does the playful use of different masks, made of diverse material, shape, and color affect the internal and external perception of the body wearing such a mask? For the experiments on bodies with plenty of faces, I gave the performer a combination of questions and material (masks, but also other objects). The general task in all of the following experiments was to physically deal with the given material and then use

---

34 For concrete examples how cultic masks were used, cf. Belting (2014), p. 44 ff.
35 Cf. Belting (2014), p. 51.
36 Cf. Belting (2014), p. 14.

it to search for possible answers to the questions. Below I will reflect on three practices developed in the course of the artistic research process that derived from playing with masks as a tool with which to perform self-distancing.

6.4.1 The practice of vanishing

The first practice I want to introduce could be labeled as a practice of vanishing. In order to reflect on this practice, I am going to look in detail at two experiments.

> Experiment
> Material set up: six different masks positioned in a half circle on the floor. Imagine these masks are additional faces. Action: put on and take off these different faces, while never showing your "own" face.

In comparison to the practices already developed when appropriating the scores built from unfamiliar labels and descriptions in the first research process[37] or when playing with the functions of the own face[38], the experiment above showed one fundamental difference to those practices. This difference resulted from the fact that the masks were external material objects existing on their own. Accordingly, the experiment confronted Vania Rovisco with external objects that could be used as external layers to be put on and taken off the body and face at will. During the experiment, the exploration of the masks as additional layers that can actually be placed on top of the body, created, in Rovisco's internal perception as a performer, the association of covering, protecting, or even shielding the own face and body. That is why one can say that the process of appropriating the masks strongly affected the particular relationship with the outside space, including me as the spectator witnessing the experiment. In this regard, one could claim that in the context of the experiment, the masks served the function of a barrier which Rovisco could put up between her own face and body and my gaze as a spectator.

Interestingly, from Rovisco's internal perspective of shielding her face with the mask while making it vanish was mostly perceived as something exciting, playful, and enjoyable. When reflecting on her experiences after the experiment Rovisco stated that during the experiment, she perceived the masks in

---

37 Cf. p. 82ff. of this paper.
38 Cf. p. 143ff. of this paper.

very diverse ways, such as a protection shield, as a neutral surface my body can hide behind, or just as waste material she had to carry. During the course of the experiment, more and more she imagined herself as a carrier of faces, not having one singular face, but having plenty of faces around her. Rovisco stated that during the experiment she enjoyed the feeling of being there and not being there at the same time. Taking Rovisco's experience to another level one can state that this practice of using the mask as a tool employed to make the individual face vanish created a feeling of agency, since the mask had created the temporary opportunity to blur the own identity by letting the own facial expressions or particular body parts disappear at will.

Simultaneously it became clear that this self-determined action of making the own face vanish had changed Rovisco's own self-perception. In this sense, the practice of making a face vanish, which in our experiment had led to a joy and pleasure of disappearing as a recognizable individual subject, could also be used as an interesting practice to question or even to subvert the concept of the body as an identity project.

Interestingly, from my outside perspective as the spectator, I perceived the practice of allowing the own individual face to vanish in a much more ambivalent way. From my outside perspective, the practice of making the individual face vanish, created difficulty at identification, and this difficulty in turn led to a feeling of alienation and a sense of witnessing something uncanny. I would like to suggest that this alienation was facilitated by the combination of two factors, on the one hand the refusal to show the "own" face and thereby the refusal to be identified, and on the other hand the simultaneous use of the own body as a space that can be carry a multitude of alternative faces.

Because of this combination, I could not engage in any act of identification and consequently experienced a state of disorientation regarding the question of the subject with which I was confronted. In the reflection on the experiment, I looked upon my feeling of insecurity and alienation as an interesting reaction to the produced self-distancing. In the following, I will analyze another practical experiment dealing with the blind spot in the face, in order to reflect on this particular state of disorientation.

Experiment
Question: Can the relationship between the subject and the act of surveillance be subverted even if there is no escape from that surveillance? In other words, how can one refuse to be identified without necessarily needing to actually disappear physically? Material: two different latex-masks and a pen.

In the experiment above, Rovisco worked with the two questions and the latex-mask and pen. Rovisco started the experiment by putting the latex-mask on her face, which from the outside perspective looked like a layer of skin in place of the usual eyes, nose and mouth. In the beginning of the experiment, Rovisco sat on the floor, while her body was still. From this quiet state, she suddenly started hitting the floor with the pen, creating a rhythm that gradually became faster and faster. In the course of the experiment Rovisco transformed the beating of the floor into a repetitive movement in space, producing a high level of energy and tension in her body that was only interrupted by short breaks in between. The strong, almost violent assumed intention behind the movement simultaneously affected me as a spectator by both creating a feeling of stress in my own body and also creating a wish to understand the purpose of all the effort witnessed. Was she only playing with abstract movement and rhythm? Or was there any concrete aim in the movement? While I was experiencing the strong wish to understand the intention of the body movement with which I was confronted, my gaze consistently moved back to the performer's face. However, in the place where the face was supposed to be, there was just a void, a plain surface of latex that prevented me from reading Rovisco's facial expressions. Thus, as an observer, I could not relate to Rovisco's face as a communication tool for her intentions.

The performative strategy used by Rovisco in order to refuse clear identification could be described as twofold, using physical movement that would build up increasing tension and simultaneously refusing to lay open the intention of that particular use of movement by making the face vanish. From the external perspective, the perceived void brought about by the latex mask created a constant irritation: was I witnessing an aggressive action, an accusation, an invitation, or simply abstract movement? Since these questions remained unanswered, as a spectator I was unable to define the particular relationship between me, as the spectator, and the body I was observing. This impossibility in turn produced in me a state of constant uncertainty and also a sense of the uncanny, while I perceived Rovisco's body as erratic. Relating my experience to Gadamer's thoughts on play, one could state that those experiences were framed by what Gadamer called the ambivalent relation to what is serious. Of course, as an observer, I knew that it was an artistic experiment without serious danger. This knowledge, however, did not prevent me from feeling irritated or even threatened by the perceived body.

6. The second artistic research project "Let's face it!" 155

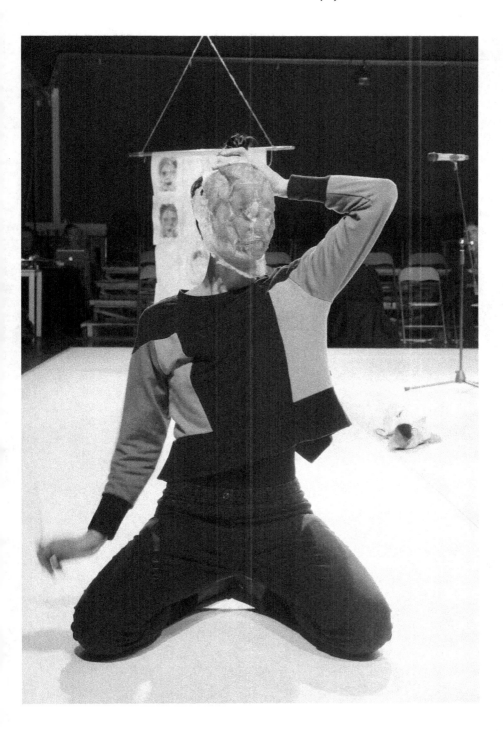

The body created here, within the research process, we called the anarchist. Although this process of labeling was rather intuitive, later reflecting on this experiment revealed an interesting outcome: A body creating a high level of physical intensity through its movements while at the same time refusing to expose its face undermines a very fundamental social rule in Western society, namely the rule that the face has to be a reference point, identifiable and recognizable for whomever one is confronted. In this regard, the practice of making the own face vanish refuses people their right to read and also to react to a person, and to try and make that person adjust to one's own intention. Relating the insights and experiences of this experiment to Butler's definition of a subject that is constituted through two relations, namely through being addressed by another person and by being able of addressing others, the reason for the irritation becomes clear. As an observer, I was clearly addressed by Rovisco's actions, but I could hardly address her, since the intentions of her actions stayed obscure. Applying the insights of this experiment to a social situation, the friction becomes even more problematic. An individual who refuses to show its own face cannot be identified as a legal person and thus can hardly be blamed for the own actions. Therefore, vanishing as a recognizable subject and not laying open the own intentions surely has an anarchist potential which might not only irritate on an individual level, but also has the potential of undermining and subverting political and institutional power structures.

One can conclude that within the artistic research process the practice of making the own face vanish used the mask as a tool to consciously blur one's own intentions and the own readability. This is why that practice also touched on the topic of agency. This topic of agency explains why the practice of making the individual face vanish produced such different feelings and associations – inside the performer as well as from someone's outside perspective. The joy and playfulness perceived from the internal perspective of the performer resulted from her experience of becoming able to actively control and blur identification in a self-determined way. The external perception of the spectator can be considered to be the opposite to this phenomenon, since the self-determined practice of vanishing necessarily confronted the spectator with the loss of control and the experience of uncertainty.

Reflecting on the practice of making the individual face disappear on a social level also raises political questions. In our Western society, who is allowed to let or even actively make one's own face become invisible? In our social context, what are possible occasions that allow for that to happen? What reactions do bodies that refuse to show their individual face evoke?

Connecting the experience of our artistic experiment for example with the discussion about prohibiting the niqab in public space, the niqab being a particular female Muslim clothing covering the whole face, one touches on interesting questions regarding Western contemporary society, namely how this society deals with the states of disorientation regarding the question of identity. Since for the reasons described above, an intentionally hidden face might create insecurity and even unease in the person with whom it is confronted, on a social level, it is interesting to ask oneself why particular groups in Western contemporary society, such as, Muslim women wearing niqabs or protesters wearing black balaclavas are much more likely to be perceived as strange or unusual whereas, for example, masked people during carnival are mostly perceived as behaving in a very light and easy-going way. It seems that the individual reaction to the masked face is a result of preconceived assumptions, not knowledge, of what the intentions of the mask-bearer are: creating amusement in the case of the masked carnival attendee or being perceived as a potential risk in the case of the masked protesters and the women wearing niqabs. As in our experiment, it is the body language accompanying the masked face that will decide on the intensity of the spectator's inner objection to the mask.

6.4.2 The practice of perceptual transformation

In my previous reflection on the practice of vanishing, I was interested in the mask as a tool to shield the own face from the spectator's gaze and by doing so to consciously produce a feeling of strangeness or mysteriousness and, ultimately, alienation in the spectator. In this context, the mask became a tool used in a self-determined way to place the spectator at a distance from the own face and body. In the following, I will reflect on another practice we developed when researching on the mask as a tool employed to play with self-distancing. This practice was built on using the mask as a tool to transform the performer's internal perception of the face and body.

Experiment:
Thinking of making the own face vanish: would you rather become an animal or a plant? How would you disguise yourself? Where would you go? Material: One empty, featureless face made of hard plaster that is covered by a wig and has been put on a tripod. One hairy mask put on the performer's face after half of the experiment.

In the experiment above, the action of putting on a particular mask provoked a very intense experience which implied a drastic transformation of Rovisco's internal physical and emotional perception. This transformation of her physical and emotional perception made it possible to temporarily step out of her known self-perceptions to appropriate an imagined fictitious plant's perception. How did this work on a concrete level? In order to reflect on Rovisco's internal experience in the frame of the experiment, I extracted some of her verbal description of her internal experience shared with me after the experiment.

> "The moment the hairy mask was put on my face, internally I connected it with the ritual masks that were used to transform people. At this moment, I felt that I got permission, I got an access to something else and it developed into bringing things into the present, like a gateway. It was funny, because it was not so much about human nature, but more about nature's faces. It converted to nature's physicality and nature's temperament rather than human. I felt like having various faces, animal faces, plant faces, a plant voice."[39]

Although, unlike in many cults and spiritual cultures, in the Western contemporary society, most individuals are not used to cultural practices of using masks as a tool to make one's own body become a medium for something or someone else, at first sight, Rovisco's internal perception of the experience had similarities to some cultic use of masks. It is likely that one could also explain her associations to the cultic use with the external features of the mask with its hair and outward appearance.

However, what was interesting was that Rovisco's description was not a mere representation of her theoretical knowledge about cultural rituals or clichés; to be more precise, what she described was an intense experience that she had had during the experiment. Consequently one could say that even without coming from the cultural background that uses masks as a tool for spiritual and perceptual transformation, in the frame of the artistic experiment the performer discovered the mask as a gateway to step outside the known ways of perception. How and to what extent was Rovisco's perception transformed, then?

---

39 This text was transcribed from a video-documented talk we had after the experiment.

6. The second artistic research project "Let's face it!" 163

"I saw trees that are ripped out of the earth, or the heavy destruction.... Things like that came up in my imagination while being there. There was one thing that was cool, in the sense of dynamic. Because it comes from nature, things that happen are not defined as good or bad, but rather as potency of energy. A hurricane is not bad it is just a lot of energy. A stream is not soft, because if a stream keeps on going, it can create as much destruction as a hurricane. It was interesting to shift my perspective and not always going through a human relation or perception. If one let go of the human perspective it becomes possible to see things in a different way, such as the manifestation of energy. That is all. We don't have to connect it to anything else. We just have to be in the present physicality of what it is. And let it go. For example, when I was doing the movement with the feet, I felt it could go further, that it was just the beginning...like an earthquake some things in nature go chaotic, but it has a quality, it is reacting towards things."[40]

Rovisco's descriptions of her internal perceptions indicate how drastically, by using the mask as a gateway, her internal experiences changed, but also her perception of the external environment. Rovisco seemed to have experienced the experiment as stepping into a fictitious plant perspective, which in her particular case meant that she had perceived everything as a pure manifestation of physical energy and hadn't even felt the need to label or evaluate the things that she had perceived.

Obviously, what Rovisco's experience cannot be understood as the perception of a real plant. The interesting aspect of her experience is in fact a different one; it is the opportunity of temporarily stepping out of the known and stepping into an unknown way of perceiving the body and the environment, which in turn enabled a vivid imagined word.

Why can one consider this experience to be so valuable? On a meta level, one could conclude that with her practicing and experiencing this fictitious plant's perception, Rovisco also practiced another skill, that of empathy with beings and objects that are fundamentally different from the own human body. In Rovisco's case, the frame of the experiment opened up the chance of perceiving the own body and the environment from a non-human, even non-individual

---

40   This text was transcribed from a video-documented talk we had after the experiment.

perspective, which could probably be considered to be a perspective different from the body as an identity project.[41]

6.4.3 The practice of playfully falling into and out of faces

Until now, in my reflection on the mask as a tool with which to create self-distancing, I focused on two possibilities; firstly, the possibility of making the individual face vanish and thereby creating a distance between the performer and the observer and, secondly, the possibility of perceptual transformation which enables the subject to experience the own self in a radically different way. In the following, I will reflect on a third possibility, which derived from a practice, which in the research process was called "falling into and falling out of faces".

In the practice "falling into and falling out of faces", I put the focus on the mask as an additional object or layer that can be put on and off the face. In the practice of "falling in and out of faces", I was interested in exploring the different consequences resulting from different ways of dealing with the mask as an external object. Accordingly, I focused on the practical actions of putting the mask on the face and taking it off again.

> Experiment:
> Material: one white cardboard mask with photo imprints of Vania's profile.
> Movement score: Research on a dialogue between the head and the mask by playing with two different activities. 1: Head moves towards the mask and away from the mask. 2: The mask led by the hand, moves toward and away from the head. Time: play with different speeds and rhythms. Spatial setup: use all 27 points in your surrounding 3 dimensional space.

Initially, from the perspective of the performer, the experiment challenged Vania Rovisco in a rather technical way. On the one level, the performed movements were supposed to constantly change spatial orientation inside all of the

---

41 In the research process, this experiment led to a further exploration of plant movement.

27 points[42] in space, while, on the other level, ways of dealing with the mask simultaneously had to be constantly altered too. The changes in dealing with the mask required that either the face approached the mask or the face removed itself from the mask, or, with the face in a static position and the mask moving, the mask approached the face or the mask removed itself from the face.

Although, from the internal perspective, the experiment led to quite an abstract and technical approach in physical movement, from the outside perspective of witnessing the experiment as an observer, the exploration of different connections between the face and the mask produced associations with all kinds of questions regarding identity.

What I perceived while witnessing the changing technical connections between the face and the mask from outside was a mask being pushed on the face, like in a violation. I saw a mask that seemed to be glued onto the face. I saw a mask that was carefully moved away from the head as if it was being used as a mirror. I saw a head removing itself from a mask and then slowly slipping back into the mask as if it was a safe and clandestine space. I saw a head falling into a mask almost like a relief and I saw a mask guiding the face through the surrounding space.

While I was watching the experiment from the external perspective, I suddenly perceived the mask not as the simple cardboard mask any more; rather I perceived it as a representation of all the different roles the body is playing in daily life, such as that of being a woman, for example, that of being an artist, a mother, a choreographer, a lover, a dancer, a friend, an intellectual, a writer, a citizen, etc. When we assume that each of those different roles implies a different perception and also use of the own body, the concept of the body as an identity project raises the question of how all of those different roles exist simultaneously. Watching this abstract movement experiment of putting on and taking off a cardboard mask, I started to ask myself how much agency an individual actually has in adopting or, alternatively, rejecting all those different roles our body carries for potential use. Considering the body to be a carrier of different roles, how easily can one step into or adopt a particular role and step out of it or reject it again? How consciously can one deal and play with all the roles one performs?

---

42 This particular spatial model of a 3dimensional cube with three levels, each of them having nine points derives from Rudolf Laban's geometrical model of space that surrounds the dancer. Compare also Forsythe, William: Improvisation Technologies. A tool for the analytical dance eye.

Relating those questions back to the thesis I discussed in chapter 4.7 on the method-acting technique,[43] namely that every individual has a public persona[44], i.e., one or rather several roles or masks each expressing one part of the individual self, I would like to raise the following question: How would our understanding of the body as an identity project change if one started to think of those roles not as something that particularly characterizes us as individual subjects, but as something that one could 'put on' and 'take off' like a mask, that one could playfully fall into and fall out of. In this thought experiment, the practice of "falling into and falling out of faces" would also imply something that could happen at random or spontaneously, without previous planning, without aiming at it beforehand, without making an effort to achieve it, yet that one would need to deal with when it actually happens.

Within the research process, the question arose of how to transfer the practice of playfully falling into and out of faces to the whole body, i.e. what kind of bodily mask we could playfully fall into and out of? In order to develop the experiment further, Rovisco proposed the task that putting the mask on the face should go together with falling into a spontaneous bodily mask, a bodily mask created by "quoting" a dance style or a particular physical state. While, from the internal perspective, this additional task even made the experiment more challenging, from the outside perspective, the results were interesting and also funny to watch. Suddenly, within the whole negotiation between head and mask, there were moments when head and mask were touching each other and simultaneously a ballet quote was created, or a Pina Bausch[45] quote, a Martha Graham[46] quote, a Marilyn Monroe quote, and also movements taken from a memory of sensory perception, such as being bullied, the feeling of floating, of itching, or of suffering from vertigo, etc.

Looking upon this experiment as one possible draft of a body with plenty of faces and asking what kind of subject is created through this experiment, one could conclude that this experiment created a subject that resides inside an ongoing negotiation of falling into and falling out of (bodily) masks. This practice put the emphasis on the constant transitions, and not on the states

---

43 Cf. chapter 4.7. of this paper
44 Cf. Batson (2007), p. 31ff.
45 Pina Bausch (1940–2009) was a German dancer and choreographer. From 1973 to 2009 Bausch was the artistic director of Tanztheater Wuppertal.
46 Martha Graham (1894–1991) was an American Modern dancer and choreographer who developed a particular movement technique called Graham technique.

themselves. Therefore, I conclude that the mask as an external object never entirely becoming a part of the own body always hints at the potential of change and development. This phenomenon, in turn, also affects the perception of the own body, since the internal body images as well as the roles the body is representing are here perceived as being in a process of constant transition.

From Rovisco's internal perspective, the practice of falling into and falling out of faces was perceived in rather an ambivalent way. On the one hand, Rovisco enjoyed the feeling of agency and freedom that went along with the practice. Simultaneously, the experiment also created a state of exhaustion in Rovisco, since no state could ever be experienced to its fullest and there were hardly any moments of rest.

From my outside perspective, this experiment produced a subject that seemed to have access to a huge archive of physical knowledge of bodily sensations as well as a dance style repertoire that it could easily put to use. This is why watching the experiment was also quite impressive, since the continuous practice of falling into and falling out of faces as well as physical movement demanded very quick transitions. On the other hand, in my role as spectator, it was impossible to say what kind of subject I was confronted with. Accordingly, this playfulness of falling into and falling out of faces gave rise to the very different perception of an individual subject that could be described as a subject putting on and taking off different potential layers, without any of these layers being more particular or matching more with the individual self-image.

6.5 Conclusion – Second research project

Having completed this whole research process of experimenting with different potentials of the face, one can conclude that the playing with the potentials of the face revealed an interesting insight into the relationship between what is known and what is unknown, or in other words, what an individual thinks and feels the individual body is and what it is not. In the experiments on a face without a body, the research started from the known terrain of what the face can do – and surprisingly, simply by detaching the actions of the face from their known function, we discovered alternative facial potentials, such as those of becoming leaking holes, plain surfaces, or musical instruments, for example.

In the experiments on a body with plenty of faces, the masks became tools with which to create a blank spot in the body image. For the external perspective of the spectator, this blank spot led to a difficulty in reading the body's intention, which in turn created different forms of irritation with regard to what kind of subject the spectator was being confronted with. From the internal perspective of the performer, this blank spot set in motion complex processes of imagining the own face and body in unfamiliar, or even fictitious ways, which in turn affected the performer's own self-perception as well as the relationship to the surrounding environment.

Also, one can conclude that, during the practical experiments, dealing with the masks fostered the development of particular practices – 1. the practice of vanishing; 2. the practice of empathy; 3. the practice of transitioning. Although all three practices focus on very different aspects, I claim that they have something in common. Taking the three practices of vanishing, empathy, and transitioning to a more general level and asking what exactly it was that was practiced in all of those three practices, one could claim that the aim was certainly not to practice a performer's own individual self-expression. In fact, what was actually practiced could be described as a skill and also a willingness to play with destabilizing the individual self- and body-image without having any preset expectation of where this process of playing might lead to.

This engagement in the playing process, which Gadamer also describes as a risk of being played and being mastered by the play, required a particular stance over the own body, i.e., a stance that required the openness and the courage to allow the own body and face to become something that one cannot fully control and plan beforehand. In the context of the artistic experiments this process was connected to an interest in surprises and coincidences. By appropriating a wide variety of faces, the artistic experiments examined the boundaries between identification and alienation, between subject and object, between having a face and having no face.

6.6 Sharing the second research project with an audience[47]

The fact that for the research process I received project funding from the City of Cologne, at some point made it necessary for me to think about how to present the outcome of our artistic research in form of a choreographic work. In other words, how could all those potential faces and bodies that we had built dur-

---

47 For the video documentation cf. https://vimeo.com/219288042

ing the research be considered choreographic material from which to create a performance?

At first, the question of how to handle this amount of very diverse material appeared to be a bit overwhelming. However, when I reflected on the research process and the particular approach of not presetting our expectations as to what kind of faces and bodies the experiments would lead to, I came to the conclusion that it made very much sense not to choreographically "curate" with regard to the faces and bodies that had arisen from the experiments. Instead, I considered all of them as potential "layers" of faces and also bodies that would be used to create a solo performance for Vania Rovisco.

After having decided that layering would be a central method in order to choreographically approach the huge variety of faces and body images that had been developed during the research, the question arising next was how to move from one of the layers to the next. With regard to the internal perspective of the performer, this question was mostly connected to her inner experience: What was her inner motivation to switch from one layer to another? What exactly would change at the moment of transition? On a formal compositional level, the question of how to move from one body image to another was also linked up with questions regarding the use of temporality and rhythm: Does the transition work for the performer when there is an abrupt change, such as a jump, or is a gradual process of morphing preferable, or is a transition something that needs to be gradually developed and constructed through a number of in-between steps?

Playing with these different ways of moving from one of the different layers to the next, actually became the basic compositional tool for the choreographic structure. What turned out to be particularly interesting in this work were the moments of transition themselves. What I aimed at was to use those compositional tools of gradual transitions and, alternatively, abrupt cuts, to leave the audience in a constant state of uncertainty about with whom they would be confronted.

A space structured in layers

In order to transfer the concept of layering into the actual performance space, it made sense to also think of the space not as of one entity, but rather as a space structured in layers. Similar to the hanging paper walls that were also creating several layers in space, I decided to position the audience as layers in space as well. Accordingly, they were sitting on two sides of the stage space and opposite to each other, like brackets. Thus, the layers of the space could be described as: audience – stage – audience, while the stage itself was structured through layers of paper walls.

This spatial structure affected the audience's perception since whatever a member of the audience perceived the activities on stage they was perceived in front of another layer, namely the audience sitting on the opposite side of the space. Through this spatial setup, during the whole performance, the audience in a way saw itself mirrored.

While Rovisco constantly worked on transitioning between all kinds of different facial layers, there always was, behind all these changes, one layer of audience faces. In my conceptual thinking about the spatial structure, I assumed that this particular spatial setup would lead to the situation that, as a spectator sitting in one half of the audience, the audience's gaze and thoughts during the performance started to also wander over to the faces in the other audience. What did they express? How different were they from the face the performer had just put on at a particular moment? At the same time, the faces in the audience could also potentially be perceived as reference faces that were looked at for their relation to the performer's face.

Choreographic structure

In the development of the choreographic piece "Let's face it!", I thought of how the interest in layering faces and, in the process of layering, also temporarily vanishing as a subject could be linked up with the social issue of surveillance and control, i.e., surveillance through facial recognition software in public spaces. When linking the results and experiences of the artistic experiments with this issue, I became interested in considering the experiments as a rehearsal of possible performative strategies that could be used as reactions to this phenomenon. Thinking this further, I conceived the theater space as a fictitious space in which the performer and also the audience would be confronted with different forms of control and surveillance.

Thus, for the choreographic piece of "Let's face it!", I thought of the theater space as a fictitious social microcosm, where each individual inside was potentially observed and surveilled. This concept, in turn, led the focus to particular questions such as, for example: Who is observed and surveilled by whom? How does one protect oneself against an observing gaze? How can one play with strategies of blurring one's own identification?

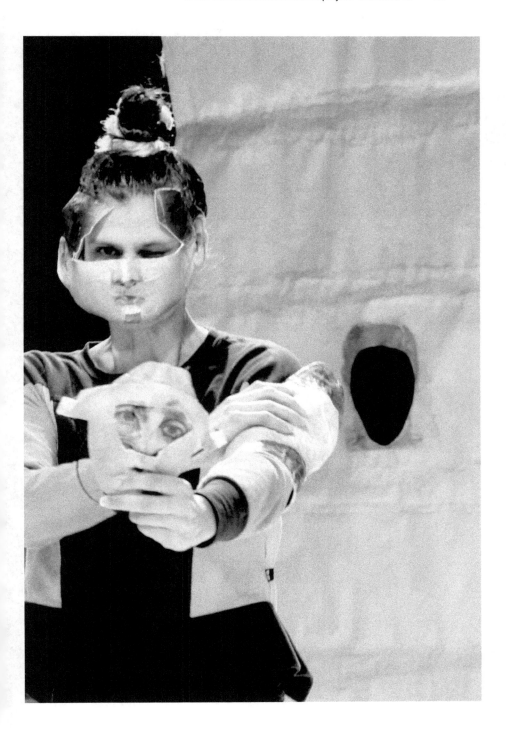

178　Antje Velsinger: The Bodies We Are (Not)

This focus obviously affected the relationship between the performer and the audience. Usually, in theater, it is the performer onstage who is observed by the audience's gaze, while in most cases the audience is not perceived as made up of individuals, but they blend into a mostly anonymous group. Therefore, in a classical theater set up the audience is observing while being invisible themselves.

In the following, I will roughly sketch the choreographic structure of "Let's face it!" in order to show how, during the course of the performance, the performer moved through different body images and facial layers. Since each of them was related to different movement material, different sensations and imaginations, different intentions as well as to different relationships with the audience, moving through all of them demanded that the performer transition between very diverse self-perceptions. Thus, also the audience was confronted with very different perceptions of one single body.

PLANT BODY
* Slowly pulsating light and sound create an atmosphere of a fictitious space in nature
* Darkness, the audience can hardly see anything
* Body without human shape and without a face.
* Plant movement
* Audience can observe while staying invisible

SOLDIER BODY
* Bright space
* Space is considered to be potentially hostile
* Paper masks are used as shields
* Defensive and attacking movement
* Right eye is used and perceived as surveillance camera. Gaze can zoom in and out.
* Audience is directly observed by the performer's gaze
* Audience is verbally addressed by the performer: "My only desire is to protect you from yourself. To protect your loved ones. Your dog. No data will be erased. I noticed that you were 15 minutes late this morning. My only desire

is to protect all you have, all you need. For your own security, no data will be destroyed."[48]

ANARCHIST BODY
* Latex-mask transforms the face into a surface without openings
* Different strategies of physically creating tension in the body through movement and rhythm without ever fully releasing this tension
* Addressing the audience through gestures of pointing without revealing the own intention
* Using the voice to produce (dark, gurgling) sounds directed at the audience

RILKE BODY
* walking up and down the stage with one hand holding the face
while addressing the audience with a text by Rilke:
Es gibt eine Menge Menschen, aber noch mehr Gesichter, denn jeder hat mehrere. Da sind Leute, die tragen ihr Gesicht jahrelang, natürlich nutzt es sich ab, und es weitet sich wie Handschuhe, die man auf der Reise getragen hat. Nun fragt es sich freilich, da sie mehrere Gesichter haben, was tun sie mit den anderen? Sie heben sie auf. Ihre Kinder sollen sie tragen. Aber vielleicht geht auch der Hund damit raus. Weshalb auch nicht? Andere Leute setzen unheimlich schnell ihre Gesichter auf, eins nach dem anderen, und tragen sie ab. Mit kaum 40 sind sie schon beim letzten. Sie sind nicht gewohnt, Gesichter zu schonen, ihr letztes ist in acht Tagen durch, hat Löcher (...) und da kommt dann nach und nach die Unterlage heraus, das Nichtgesicht, und sie gehen damit herum.[49]

There are great many people, but there are even more faces because each person has several. There are those who wear one face years on end; naturally, it starts to wear, it becomes stretched like gloves that are kept for traveling. Admittedly, since they have several faces, the question now arises: what do they do with

---

48　The text was generated in the artistic experiments when exploring the particular interests and desires that were related to the particular body image of the soldier.
49　Cf. Schmidt Bergmann (ed.) (2000), p. 11f.

the others? They save them. They'll do for the children. There have even been instances when dogs have gone out with them on. And why not? A face is a face. Other people change their faces one after the other with uncanny speed and wear them out. Before they are even forty they're down to the last of them. They are not used to looking after faces; their last one wore through in a week and has holes in it and in many places it's as thin as paper; bit by bit the bottom layer, the non-face, shows through and they go about wearing that.[50]

PLAIN PAPER WALL FACE (1)
* The performer's face becomes a surface on a paper wall, one of many copies.
* Opening and closing the eyes without directly addressing the audience
* Surreal atmosphere supported by lighting and music

FALLING INTO AND OUT OF FACES
* Performing different movement relationships between head and mask
* Falling into and out of bodily quotes of dance-styles as well as those of physical sensations
* Performing gestures that demonstrate power
* Addressing the audience with the help of language
by verbally improvising with the following text:
I see you, I observe you, I surveil you, I observe and have ensured an intimate space for your comfort and protection. I have installed a new system that now detects heat, nervous reactions, abrupt audio pitches.... and that has the capacity to penetrate clothing by using X-ray technology. I do this for your security. I surveil your children, your dog at all times. I see that you feel protected. I see that you are changing your hairstyle very often these days. Smile, you are being watched. You observe me? You watch me? You surveil me, you see me, you observe me – I surveil you, I see you , I observe you. No data will be erased. 24/7 surveillance for your protection. CCTV LRDS ? with your permission.

---

50   Cf. Rilke, Rainer Maria; Needham, William (2013) Die Aufzeichnung des (The Notebook of) Malte Laurids Brigge – Vol.1 (of 2) (German English Bilingual Edition)

PLAIN PAPER WALL FACE (2)
* The performer's face becomes a surface on a paper wall, one of many copies.
* Opening and closing the eyes without directly addressing the audience
* Surreal atmosphere supported by lighting and music

LIZ BODY
* Playing with the withdrawal of the own gaze inside the own body
* Movement playing on the mouth anus connection
* Breath comes out through the mouth and circulates in the surrounding space
* The audience gets approached by the performer's breath

SATELLITE BODY
* Dark blue lighting
* Everything moves in the form of circles: a mask on a long string gets swung around the performer's head; hips and arms move, doing circles
* Intention of seducing the audience with the help of that movement
* Addressing the audience through text, while hardly being visible: We will see you. We will observe you. We will surveille you. We will protect you. We will protect your loved ones, your dog. We will install CCTV systems. We will have your permission. You will give us your permission. We will ensure that you have space for your comfort. We will constantly watch your children. Your dog. We will be there to protect you.
* Putting on a furry mask and slowly leaving the stage

6. The second artistic research project "Let's face it!"

6.7 Reflections on the utopian potential of playing with self-distancing

By assembling all those different layers of faces and body images in a choreographic structure, in "Let's face it!", Rovisco performed diverse temporal versions of her own self, such as a plant body, a soldier body, an anarchist body, a Rilke body, a plain paper wall face, a body with manifold faces, a Liz body, or a satellite body. Rovisco's performance of those different body images facilitated radical changes in how her body and face were perceived from the internal as well as from the external perspective. Thus, during the course of the performance, Rovisco practiced manifold transformations of her internal and external body image.

Reflecting on Rovisco's particular attitude to her body, one could state that, in "Let's face it!", Rovisco applied various strategies of self-distancing to experience otherness in her body. Thinking about otherness and self-distancing also points at another issue – the psychological risk of losing the oneself. As our research showed, practicing self-distancing led to the experience of other physical as well as emotional territory. How, then, is this practice of playfully creating distance to one's own self different from states of psychological disorder? I state that the difference is in the degree of agency. While losing one's own self as a result of a psychological or physical disorder is no voluntary choice, the practice of playing with the destabilization of known self- and body-images, as referred to here, is a voluntary act which can be used to question familiar ideas and received truths regarding the own body and self.

Obviously, playfully creating distance to the own self is much easier in a choreographic context than in daily social life. However, when looking for ways to emancipate the body from the social imperative of optimization and control, I propose that practicing self-distancing could also be helpful outside of the choreographic context. As the artistic research project has shown, the practice of self-distancing is connected to a particular attitude toward the individual body. This attitude is both playful and risk-taking since it allows experimenting with the body without pre-deciding on the results. As such, this attitude radically differs from what Villa describes as hard work[51] in order to achieve the goal of an optimized self. In contrast to the goal oriented and rather serious work on the body, in the context of the artistic experiments, play facilitated a serious and simultaneously non-serious approach to the body. Playing with

---

51   Cf. Villa (2008b), p. 260.

the deconstruction and reconstruction of diverse body images produced unexpected results. It produced body images the performers personally did not relate to before the experiment.

Thus, playing with different strategies of self-distancing leads to a particular understanding of the body in which the body is not exclusively considered as the expression of an individual identity. When I state that playing with self-distancing could be a powerful strategy to emancipate the body from the social imperative of self-optimization, I assume that letting go of the belief in the body as an identity project potentially creates a relief. The moment the body is not considered as the representative of an ideal self, the neoliberal request for self-enhancement could not affect the individual relation to the body in such a radical way.

When reflecting on the insights of the artistic research process and transferring those insights to the neoliberal social context outside the artistic field, in my opinion, using the body as a place and medium for practicing self-distancing even implies a utopian[52] potential. In my opinion, the utopian potential lies in the fact that playing with self-distancing focuses on the exact opposite of self-optimization and control: taking risks, allowing oneself to become affected by something one cannot fully control, practicing empathy with the other, becoming engaged without expectation. Applying the insights of the artistic research process on the social context outside the field of art, I imagine that the more individuals would practice not using the body as an identity project, i.e., as a place with which to increase one's own value, the easier it could become to also integrate those physical phenomena which the logic of self-optimization must reject.

From a utopian perspective, re-learning to play with self-distancing in the neoliberal social context could mean stopping the constant effort to achieve self-expression, self-development, and self-enhancement and, instead, starting to allow the unfamiliar, the strange and the vulnerable potentials of the body to take up more room. Maybe, relearning to play with self-distancing could create more humor, or it could lead to becoming better at feeling and

---

52   The utopian potential I am reflecting on here is not connected to a defined draft of one particular future body. I detect this utopian potential in playfully practicing self-distance as a strategy to practically react to problems or frictions that have arisen from the present social role of the body by rehearsing alternative ways of being in and with the body. Cf. also Seel, Martin (2001) Drei Regeln für Utopisten.

also at showing empathy with those we usually tend to reject, ignore, or forget. Maybe, relearning to play with self-distancing could help individuals to include all those layers in them that, usually, are excluded as being too vulnerable, too menacing, or simply too different. Maybe relearning to practice self-distancing could enable individuals to also use alternative body-images to enrich their field of perceptions and skills. Maybe those skills and alternative ways of perception, such as expanding, becoming anonymous or switching to a plant perception, might also be helpful in different situations of their everyday lives.

One might raise the critical question where individuals outside the artistic field can find opportunities to practice self-distancing. Maybe practicing self-distancing could begin with searching for moments in the everyday life in which the own body can be used and perceived in a yet unfamiliar way. A possible starting point could be the following task.

Experiment:

Call a friend and make an appointment to go for a walk for one hour. When you meet this friend, take his/her hand and tell him/her that, for the next hour, you will walk hand in hand and walk backwards without talking to each other. While you are doing this silent backwards walk, keep note of everything that comes to your mind. How, for example, is this unfamiliar way of moving through your environment changing the perception of your own body? How is it affecting your relationship to space and to time? How is it affecting your thoughts about the relationship to your friend? How is it affecting your associations regarding particular things in life that you want to achieve? While moving in this unfamiliar way, what comes to your mind when thinking about things you urgently want to achieve? Take and keep note of as many details as you can, and invite your associations with this physical experience. After one hour, sit down and silently write down every thought and association you remember having had during the walk. And then share them with your friend.

7. Conclusion

The opening premise of my thesis was the observation that, within Western neoliberal society, the body is increasingly understood and used as a place of self-optimization and goal- and profit-oriented work on a person's self. The critical consideration of this phenomenon raised the question of a possible other, non-optimizing and non-controlling approach to the body. This question piqued my interest as a choreographer, since I consider choreography as an artistic practice that offers the possibility not only to critically reflect on how bodies do things, but also to imagine, develop and rehearse alternative ways of being, moving, and dealing with bodies.

In the context of the present work, I have therefore sought a change of perspective on the body: If the optimization of the body in the current Western neoliberal society, especially in the career-oriented social middle class, is understood as the improvement of one's own, already known self, could the body, as a counter-position to this, perhaps be explored as a place for experimenting and becoming unfamiliar with oneself?

My research on the body as a place for becoming unfamiliar to the own self was based on the assumption that what a body or, more precisely, a body-image is and becomes is open to negotiation. Therefore, in the theoretical part of my research, I investigated various theoretical perspectives on how body images could actively be re-created. Based on Shaun Gallagher's concept of the body image, stating that the body image is built by three aspects – individual perception, conceptual construction (through language) and emotional attitude – I investigated the different aspects that take part in the construction of the body image.

With Merleau-Ponty, I investigated the body as a perceiving agent. Referring to Merleau-Ponty's thesis that the body as a subject creates its own world, including its own body, through individual perception, I pointed out that the individual can influence the internal body image by consciously making choices on how one's own body is perceived. In this context, Merleau-Ponty's thesis of a synthesis of the body's visual, tactile and motor aspects was central, stating that the individual can use visualizations of the body in order to influence the tactile perception, which, in turn, also influences the particular movements of the body.

With Butler, I examined further the potential of language as a tool to create discourse on the body. Referring to Butler's thesis that a body is a "linguistic being", I pointed out that the action of labeling and describing bodies and, in a second step, physically appropriating those labels and descriptions can be used as a tool to consciously influence the body image. While Butler's theory considers the constant repetition of familiar names and labels as an instrument of power that suppresses the body's versatility, I proposed that, in the context of my research, the process of describing and labeling bodies in yet unfamiliar ways could also be used as a creative tool to expand already existing ideas and imaginations about the body, which in turn potentially affect the perception of the body.

By discussing Hegel's thoughts about the particular relation between sensuous perception and language, I pointed out that there must always be a gap between individual perception and describing this perception with language. By discussing Schiller's notion of play, I proposed to consider this gap as a creative potential when consciously trying to create yet unfamiliar body images. As Schiller states, play can be understood as a third force that enables a playful interaction between the sensuous and the intelligible part of the individual. In play, both sensory perception and language mutually affect each other. Applying this understanding of play on Gallagher's concept of the body image, I proposed that the body image could be considered as a potential field for experimentation. In my practical artistic research, playing with the body image involved both exploring choreographic and performative strategies for creating yet unfamiliar perceptions of the body and exploring artistic strategies to create yet unfamiliar thoughts, ideas and imaginations about the body, while both processes mutually affected each other in constant negotiation.

In the first artistic research project "the bodies we are", together with a group of co-researchers that consisted of Sophie Aigner, Juli Reinartz, Johanna Roggan and Vania Rovisco, I investigated the body as a potential place to become unfamiliar with one's own self on a practical artistic level. In the beginning of the practical research, everyone in the research team contributed photos of bodies that fascinated them, but which they could not identify with on an individual level. Interestingly, most of these images showed bodies with "extreme" features in their outward appearance. Thus, what was perceived as unfamiliar or "the other" within our research group were bodies that differed in one or another way from the neoliberal ideal of a trained, healthy, young and controlled body.

In the research process, three of the collected photos were intuitively selected to work with in the practical artistic experiments: an extremely massive female body, an extremely muscular male body and a female body which triggered associations of BDSM[1] practices. The practical artistic experiments that were developed based on these images can be described as different ways of creating confrontations or frictions between familiar body images already existing in the co-researchers and those aspects of the depicted bodies the co-researchers, for individual or social reasons, did not want, allow or should not identify with.

On a practical level, this confrontation implied several steps. The first step was to use language to describe what each individual of the research group saw in the depicted bodies. From those descriptions, performative scores were generated, which were then performed by the different members of the research team. By being asked to physically perform those scores, the performers were confronted with several gaps between the actual perception of one's own body and those unfamiliar labels and descriptions that were previously ascribed to a body with which they individually did not identify.

In the artistic experiments of the first research project "The bodies we are", we developed several performative strategies to deal with those gaps. One strategy was to reduce the inner focus on only one particular aspect of the body (such as weight) and use imagination to enlarge this physical sensation and perception to its maximum. This inner focusing not only created different self-perceptions in the performers, but it also went along with discovering particular physical interests regarding the own body related to the particular focus, such as an interest and exploration of the relationship between mass, volume and the way of breathing. Focusing the individual perception to only one particular aspect of the body, in turn, also affected the particular way in which simple physical actions, such as "lifting an arm", "dancing in a club" or "jumping", were performed and experienced. In this process of physically

---

1 BDSM is a variety of often erotic practices or roleplaying involving bondage, discipline, dominance and submission, sadomasochism, and other related interpersonal dynamics.

appropriating specific names and labels, the performers translated a particular label or description into concrete physical perceptions, which led to the creation of particular movements and micro-movements that derived from this particular perception.

Another strategy that was developed to deal with the created gaps was connected to those labels that were fictitious, surrealistic or metaphorical. These generated fictitious or surrealistic labels, such as "anonymous fruit" or "human battery", were unfamiliar in a double sense. Not only were they ascribed to another body, but they also had no obvious physical counterpart in the body yet. A strategy that was developed in order to appropriate those labels was to generate particular questions that refer to possible physical details linked to those labels and to answer them directly on a performative level.

When appropriating, for example, the fictitious description "tentacles of lust", the performer could ask: What body part could be those tentacles? What movement would this body part as "tentacles of lust" do? What would those tentacles be interested in? In the process of physically exploring possible answers to those questions, the raised questions could become more and more detailed, referring to particular gestures, movements, movement qualities, intentions, but also to perceived imaginations and desires that might come up during the process of appropriation.

One can conclude that, in the practical research, re-creating the own body image implied a process of translating unfamiliar bodily labels and descriptions into associated movements and sensations that could be individually perceived in the performers' bodies. The performed movements and felt sensations, in turn, generated particular imaginations, interests and thoughts in the own body, which, in a following step, could then be re-translated into particular physical actions and sensations. Using the body as a place to become unfamiliar to the own self could therefore be described as a process of destabilizing known body- and self-images by generating alternative experiences in and thoughts on the body.

In the practical research, however, it became clear that playfully re-creating the individual body image also has its limits. In the artistic experiments, several moments occurred in which the performers felt frustrated. In those moments, the process of appropriation often remained too much on an intellectual level in which the performers could not (yet) physically translate the particular labels or descriptions of a score into performative material. The biggest problems, however, occurred in those moments when a performer could not find a personal interest in the other body. Although the applied method gave the performers the freedom to create individual scores by choosing and combining different names and labels from the pool of descriptions, there were cases in which a performer could not find an individual interest in the chosen material at all.

In retrospect, I think that there were several reasons for the occurring problems. One reason was the openness of the applied method which not only allowed for an individual approach but also, due to the absence of detailed tasks and guidance, was a challenge for the performers, since they were responsible for finding their own individual approach. From the performers' internal perspective, the reason for the occurring difficulties was described as a feeling of emotional resistance to identify with a particular body and its ascribed names and labels.

This defensiveness that occurred during different moments of the practical research process could also be related to the fact that the depicted bodies clearly differed from the neoliberal ideal of an optimized and controlled body. Thus, they were bodies with which, in the neoliberal logic of self-optimization, the members of the research group had learned not to identify. Thus, the artistic research process could also be described as an exploration of how to create interest and curiosity in those potentials of the body that are mostly excluded by the practices of optimization and control.

Being confronted with those problems, I searched for an additional approach that might offer a more detailed strategy of creating interest and curiosity in the other. For that reason, I became interested in the Method Acting Technique. By considering the performer as a "professional experiencer" who can "become" any fictitious character by immersing him- or herself in the emotional and sensory perceptions of this particular character, Method Acting lays its focus on the exact aspect that, in the previous research, partly produced problems – the emotional identification with the other.

Assuming that every character has a central emotional "need", and that identifying with the other can be achieved by finding this "need" within one's own self, Method Acting uses a question and answer technique that aims at making the performer see, hear, smell, taste and feel the fictitious world from the perspective of the other body, while putting a strong focus on the emotional experience. And indeed, when appropriating this technique, we experienced that the method was very strong in creating an emotional identification with the other. However, the particular way of asking and answering questions on a verbal level focused so much on a narrative context that the performers had difficulties to also translate their answers into physical movements.

In order to deal with this problem, I combined the Method Acting question and answer technique with a performative task to transition between the five different layers "shape", "sensation", "action", "setting", and "need", and to intuitively translate the content of one layer into another. This process of translating back and forth between the five different layers shape, sensation, action, setting, and need enabled the performer to emotionally identify with another body and to discover and experience physical aspects that were individually ascribed to the other body. This approach also made it possible to generate fragments of a fictitious past and future of the own body.

Taking the different theoretical and practical insights of the first research project "the bodies we are" into account, one can conclude that the process of appropriating details of other bodies in order to re-create one's own individual body image could be described not only as a potential leap to a different space of action and perception, but also a potential leap to different imaginations and desires with which the subject is not forced to automatically fully identify. Therefore, one could also describe this process as a rehearsal of alternative body images, as a chance for distancing oneself from what is individual and subjective.

Further considering the different insights and experiences of the research process and connecting them with my interest in proposing a perspective that differs from considering the body as an identity project, in this thesis, I proposed to consider the body as a sensitive "container". I am aware that the term container is in some respects problematic, since a body is not standardized and cannot be filled in literal ways. Nevertheless, this term seemed to be applicable, since it emphasizes the potential openness of the human body. As the research has shown, consciously "filling" the body with content must be an individual negotiation on which the subject has to agree. If this agreement is given, the body cannot only be used as a place and medium to express the individual success in fulfilling neoliberal norms and expectations; rather the body can be used to rehearse manifold, yet unknown ways of perceiving the own self as well as the surrounding environment. Expanding this further, the body as a sensitive container could therefore be regarded as a place where the self constantly finds and loses "itself".

By introducing Richard Sennett's analysis of different notions of the body in the 18th, 19th and 20th century, I pointed out that the proposal of not necessarily considering the body as something individual can also be found in the 18th century, when individuals considered the body as something impersonal as well as something natural. Based on Sennett's analysis, I pointed out that the belief in the body as an expression of the own individual identity was closely linked to the upcoming of industrial capitalism in the 19th century and its interest in the individual as a consumer. Sennett describes the negative social effect of considering the body an expression of the own identity as an excessive occupation with the own self and an incapability of dealing with the unfamiliar. According to Sennett, two capacities were lost in this development: firstly, the ability to self-distance; and secondly, the ability to play.

Thinking Sennett's request for re-practicing self-distancing and play further, in the second research project "Let's face it!", I became interested in bodies that practice self-distancing by consciously evading and blurring clear forms of identification. This focus, in turn, led to a deeper interest in the human face, since, in European culture, the face is considered the particular body part that is used as a central reference point when identifying an individual.

In the second research project "Let's face it!", I invited the performer and choreographer Vania Rovisco and the visual artist Sophie Aigner to research on the question of how to distance oneself from one's own individual face by experimenting with three fictitious body images: a face without a body, a body without a face and a body with many faces. The fact that the second artistic research project was planned as an interdisciplinary research project, including the field of choreography and visual art, led to a focus not only on the performer's body, but also on particular materials and objects that could be added onto the face and to partly or even completely let the individual face disappear.

In the experiments on a "face without the body", I researched on strategies that can be used to perceive one's own individual face in yet unfamiliar ways. In those experiments, the performer practically explored the range of potential actions and functions of the individual face, such as emotional facial expressions, sensory perception and, on a functional level, openings and closings due to muscular and joint structures. In different experiments, the possible movements and micro-movements of those different functions were considered as choreographic material. By rhythmically playing with those movements, by taking out particular elements and combining them, by zooming in on one detail and enlarging it, etc., the movements of the face were considered as choreographic material with which the performer could experiment.

This process of detaching the movements of the face from the known functions led to a perceivable change in the internal as well as external perception of the performer's faces. Distancing oneself from one's own individual face by considering its movements and functions as choreographic material made it possible to not primarily perceive one's own face as a body part that communicates individual emotions and intentions or is used for identifying an individual; rather as a body part with manifold potential functions, such as a musical instrument, a "gate" between inside and outside, a wet space that absorbs external objects and assimilates them, a camera that records the external space, etc.

Because, in the social context, the human face is an important body part for others to read and decode particular emotions as well as intentions of an individual with whom they are confronted, those experiments also strongly affected the observer. Being confronted with those other ways of using the individual face in the different artistic experiments, the observer could not fall back on socially learned strategies of reading and decoding a face, which at first produced a state of disorientation, then resulted in an active search for alternative ways of encountering the performer's face.

In the experiments on a "body with plenty of faces", I explored the use of masks as a tool to create distance from the individual face. For those experiments, visual artist Sophie Aigner first produced multiple imprints of the performer's face; made from plaster, latex, paper, etc., which could then be used as masks and enabled the performer on a practical level to experiment with different ways of layering faces and letting the own individual face disappear at will. In those experiments, three different practices were developed: the practice of letting the face vanish, the practice of perceptual transformation and the practice of falling in and out of faces.

In the practice of letting one's own face vanish, the masks were used as a tool to shield the individual face against the observer's gaze. From the internal perspective of the performer, letting the individual face disappear at will generally resulted in a feeling of excitement and agency. From the outside perspective of the observer, this practice created moments of disorientation. Being addressed by a body without being able to use the face as a reference point to read the performer's intentions created an uncanny feeling of being confronted with an erratic body that was perceived as a potential risk. The practice of letting the individual face disappear can therefore also be described as a strategy of creating a subject that addresses others while simultaneously refusing to be addressed.

In the practice of perceptual transformation, the masks were used as a tool to consciously step into other perspectives, such as that of a fictitious plant. In the practice of perceptual transformation, putting on the mask as a second facial layer inspired the performer to generate vivid imaginations which allowed her to drastically change the individual perception of the own body as well as the surrounding environment. What was practiced here was surely not an authentic plant perspective, but empathy with beings and objects that are fundamentally different from her human body.

In the practice of falling in and out of faces, the focus was on a rather technical approach to the mask as an additional object that can be put on and taken off the face. In the first version of this practice, the performer investigated different possible relations and qualities in the encounters between the face and the mask, such as a face falling into a mask, a mask being pushed onto a face, a face being slowly removed from a mask, etc. In the second version of the practice, the encounter between mask and face went together with falling into a spontaneous bodily mask, created by "quoting" a dance style or a particular physical state. This practice focused on quickly putting on and taking off different potential facial and bodily layers.

In the research process of "Let's face it!", I not only researched on how performing a body having plenty of faces, a body with no face or a face without a body can create different temporal versions of the self, but the focus was also on accumulating all those different versions of one's own self in the performer's body and practicing transitions between them. In the practical research process, this research of different transitions, such as falling in and falling out, gradually morphing, applying several in-between steps, etc., demanded from the performer to practice shifting between different imaginations, facial expressions, body tensions, movement qualities, spatial orientations, etc. Moving through the construction, de-construction, and re-construction of diverse temporal body images examined the boundaries between identification and alienation, between subject and object, between having a face and not having a face.

The two artistic research projects "the bodies we are" and "Let's face it!" have shown to what extent the choreographic field can offer the possibility to experience and use the individual body as a place to become unfamiliar with one's own self. Considering the self as a unity of the body's perceiving and reflecting dimension, one could conclude that each of those created temporal body images could be considered as a potential alternative version of one's own self. Practicing self-distancing in and with the body can therefore be described as a rehearsal of other temporal versions of the self which the performers could voluntarily enter and exit. I use the term rehearsal here to stress that those alternative versions of the self could be practiced, tested and explored without the performer necessarily identifying with them fully.

Comparing this particular attitude and use of the body to the neoliberal social context with its interest in considering the body as a place and medium for self-optimization, one can outline a fundamental difference. In the neoliberal context, using the body as a place for working on one's own self follows a pre-set ideal of the body and, therefore, working in and with the body must be considered as a highly normative work that must constantly exclude those potentials of the body that transcend this ideal. Thus, the neoliberal imperative of self-enhancement radically narrows down how bodies are potentially used and formed. By researching on choreographic strategies of self-distance, I aimed at expanding the potentials of the body beyond this logic of optimization and control. By appropriating features of those bodies with which the performers did not identify or by exploring ways to perceive one's own individual face in yet unfamiliar ways, the performer s entered states in which they could destabilize known ways of perceiving one's own body and self. This approach enabled the performers to temporarily blur the clear separation between the own and the other body, which in turn also offered a possibility of integrating bodily features that were unfamiliar or rejected before.

As the experiments have shown, practicing self-distancing not only affected the performer conducting the experiments but also affected the witnessing observer. This affection was especially strong in those moments where the observer experienced states of disorientation, since known ways of perceiving the performer's body could be disrupted. In this thesis, I discussed this particular relationship between the performer and the observer in dialogue with Gadamer's thoughts on play by pointing out that, in the artistic context, playing must be considered as something that happens "in between" the artist (doing something) and the observer (reacting to it). In retrospect, having experienced this potential of initiating alternative ways of perceiving bodies in the observer, I would have chosen to include the external perspective of the audience even more in my research.

Taking the different insights of the two research projects into account, one can conclude that what was actually practiced during the artistic research process could be described as a skill and also a willingness to play with destabilizing the individual self- and body image by taking risks, allowing oneself to become affected by something one cannot fully control, by practicing empathy with the other, by becoming engaged without expectation.

One may ask what sense and benefit there is in perceiving oneself as a lustfully expanding body, a plant-body, a permeable body, an anarchist body, a leaking hole, a surveillance camera, or as a warrior. The fact that this question cannot generally be answered unequivocally represents, in my opinion, the exact potential of this work. Perhaps, in a society in which the personal investment in one's own body should lead to the most controllable and measurable profit possible, it is precisely this openness and freedom of purpose towards the body that offers an emancipative, perhaps even utopian potential in dealing with the social demand for optimization and control of bodies.

Instead of narrowing down the ways in which a body should be used and perceived, the developed strategies of becoming unfamiliar with one's own self aimed at expanding what the individual body can be and become. As the artistic experiments have shown, the process of appropriating unfamiliar bodily features could be used to bridge the gap between what was considered to be familiar and unfamiliar. The more diverse aspects of the own body and self could be experienced, the more the clear separation between one's own self and the other got blurred, because the other might also include a potential aspect of one's own body and self. In this context, practicing self-distancing is not understood as a fixed result, but as a process of discovery.

One might critically remark that the choreographic strategies that were researched with regard to emancipating the body from the neoliberal request of self-optimization and control were only explored and tested by a small group of professional dancers and performers who, due to their individual education, were trained to use and reflect on their bodies in very conscious ways. Although I fully agree with the critical remark that, in the neoliberal social context, individuals surely have less time, space and opportunities to actively practice strategies of self-distance, this does not mean that individuals outside the artistic field cannot experiment with alternative ways of using and reflecting on their bodies.

Expanding this critical remark further, however, leads to the particular question of how individuals outside the artistic field could make use of this research. My initial question of how the choreographic field could be used to emancipate the body from the neoliberal social request of self-optimization implied the assumption that the choreographic field could be used to create other perspectives on the body. As the research process has shown, the developed strategies of self-distancing must be considered as an individual practice that has to be experienced. If, however, the developed strategies of self-distancing are based on individual practice and have to be experienced, a new question arises: Is it enough to make our individual perspectives transparent by sharing methods, insights and problems of this specific research process?

Or would it be a logical next step to create opportunities for individuals outside the artistic field to explore ways of applying our developed strategies?

After conducting this research, those questions still remain unanswered. I consider this thesis to be an open invitation for everyone interested to join the research process and relate the insights presented herein to their own research, topics and interests.

8. References

Abraham, Anke; Müller, Beatrix (2010) Körperhandeln und Körpererleben. Einführung in ein brisantes Feld. In: dies. (eds.) Körperhandeln und Körpererleben, p. 9–39 (Bielefeld: transcript).
Abraham, Anke (2010) Körpertechnologien, das Soziale und der Mensch. In: Abraham, Anke; Müller, Beatrice (eds.) Körperhandeln und Körpererleben, p. 113–139 (Bielefeld: transcript).
Alkemeyer, Thomas; Budde, Gunilla; Freist, Dagmar (eds.) (2013) Selbstbildungen. Soziale und kulturelle Praktiken der Subjektivierung (Bielefeld: transcript).
Apostolou- Hölscher (2015) Vermögende Körper. Zeitgenössischer Tanz zwischen Ästhetik und Biopolitik (Bielefeld: transcript).
Appropriation Now! Texte zur Kunst, Heft 46/2002.
Avanessian, Armen; Hester, Helen (eds) (2015) dea ex machina (Berlin: Merve Verlag).
Bardola, Nicola (ed) (2012) Utopien. Ein Lesebuch (Frankfurt a.M.: Fischer Verlag).
Batson, Susan (2007) TRUTH, personas, needs and flaws in building actors and creating characters (New York: Rugged Land).
Belting, Hans (2014) Faces. Eine Geschichte des Gesichts (München: Verlag C.H. Beck).
Beringer, Elizabeth (ed): Feldenkrais, Moshe (2010) Embodied wisdom: the collected papers of Moshe Feldenkrais (Berkeley: North Atlantic Books).
Bexte, Peter (2013) Wo immer vom Sehen die Rede ist... (München: Wilhelm Fink Verlag).
Boehm, Gottfried; Alloa, Emmanuel; Budelacci, Orlando; Wildgruber, Gerald (eds) (2014) Imagination. Suchen und Finden (Paderborn: Wilhelm Fink Verlag).

Bogart, Anne; Landau, Tina (2005) The viewpoints book. A practical guide to viewpoints and composition (New York: TCG).

Böhler, Arno; Herzog, Christian, Pechriggl (eds) (2013) Korporale Performanz. Zur bedeutungsgenerierenden Dimension des Leibes (Bielefeld: transcript).

Borgdorff, Henk (2010) Artistic Research as Boundary Work. In: Caduff, Corina; Siegenthaler, Fiona; Wälchli, Tan (eds.) Art and Artistic Research.

Brauneck, Manfred (2020) Masken – Theater, Kult und Brauchtum (Bielefeld: transcript).

Bröckling, Ulrich (2007) Das unternehmerische Selbst (Berlin: Suhrkamp).

Bublitz, Hannelore (2017) Diskurstheorie. In: Gugutzer, Robert; Klein, Gabriele; Meuser, Michael (eds). Handbuch der Körpersoziologie (Wiesbaden: Springer).

Burrows, Jonathan (2010) Scores, studios, improvisation, p. 141–151. In: A choreographer's handbook (New York: Routledge).

Butler, Judith (1991) Das Unbehagen der Geschlechter (Berlin: Suhrkamp).

Butler, Judith (1993) Bodies that matter, on the discursive limits of "sex" (New York & London: Routledge).

Butler, Judith (1997) Exitable speech: a politics of the performative. (New York: Routledge).

Butler, Judith (2001) Psyche der Macht (Berlin: Suhrkamp).

Caduff, Corina; Siegenthaler, Fiona; Wälchli, Tan (eds) (2010) Art and artistic research (Zürich: Verlag Scheidegger & Spiess).

Clarke, Gill; Cramer, Franz Anton; Müller, Gisela (2011) Gill Clarke – Minding Motion. In: Diehl, Ingo; Lampert, Friederike (ed) (2011) Dance Techniques 2010 – Tanzplan Deutschland.

Conner, Janet (2009) Writing down your soul: How to activate and listen to the extraordinary voice within (San Francisco: Conari Press).

Crossley, Nick (2001) The social body. Habit, identity and desire (London: Sage Publications).

Cvejic, Bojana (2009) Schnittverfahren und Mischungen. In: tanz-journal, May 2009.

Cwynar-Horta, Jessica (2016) The Commodification of the Body Positive Movement on Instagram. In: Stream: Inspiring Critical Thought. 8, Nr.2, p. 36–56.

Dahms, Sybille (2001) Tanz (Kassel: Bärenreiter).

Deleuze, Gilles; Guattari, Félix (1987) A thousand plateaus: capitalism and schizophrenia (London, New York: Continuum).

Denham, S. A. (1986). Social Cognition, Prosocial Behavior, and Emotion in Preschoolers: Contextual Validation. Child Development, 57(1), p. 194–201.
Diehl, Ingo; Lampert, Friederike (ed) (2011) Dance techniques 2010 – Tanzplan Deutschland (Leipzig: Henschel).
Federici, Silvia (2020) Jenseits unserer Haut. Körper als umkämpfter Ort im Kapitalismus (Münster: Unrast Verlag).
Foellmer, Susanne (2009) Am Rand der Körper. Inventuren des Unabgeschlossenen im Zeitgenössischen Tanz (Bielefeld: transcript).
Forsythe, William (2012) Improvisation Technologies. A tool for the analytical dance eye (Berlin: Hatje Cantz).
Foster, Susan (2006) Dancing Bodies. In: Desmond, Jane (ed.): Meaning in Motion. New Cultural Studies of Dance (Durham: Duke University Press).
Foucault, Michel (1978) Dispositive der Macht. Über Sexualität, Wissen und Wahrheit (Berlin: Merve).
Foucault, Michel (1981) The Order of Discourse. In: Robert Young: Untying the text: A Post-Structuralist Reader. (Boston: Routledge Kegan & Paul).
Foucault, Michel (1988) The Care of the Self. (New York: Vintage Books).
Foucault, Michel (1993) Technologien des Selbst. In: Gutman, Huck; Hutton, Patrick Foucault, Michel (2014) Die Heterotopien. Der utopische Körper (Berlin: Suhrkamp).
Gadamer, Hans-Georg (2004) Truth and Method (London, New York: Continuum).
Gallagher, Shaun (2007) How the body shapes the mind, p. 127–142. In: Philosophical Psychology. Vol. 20, No.1 (New York: Routledge, Taylor and Francis).
Gallagher, Shaun (1986) Body image and body schema. A conceptual clarification. p. 541–554. In: Journal of Mind and Behaviour, Vol. 7, No. 4.
Gallagher, Shaun; Zahavi, Dan (2012) The phenomenological mind (London, New York: Routledge).
Gebauer, Gunter (2001) Körper-Utopien. In: Merkur. Deutsche Zeitschrift für europäisches Denken. Heft 9/10. 55. Jahrgang (Stuttgard: Klett-Cotta).
Goffman, Erving (1959) The presentation of self in everyday life (New York: Anchor Books).
Gugutzer, Robert (2002) Leib, Körper, Identität (Wiesbaden: Springer).
Gugutzer, Robert (2015) Soziologie des Körpers (Bielefeld: transcript).
Haarmann, Anke (2019) Artistic Research. Eine epistemologische Ästhetik (Bielefeld: transcript).
Han, Byung-Chul (2010) Die Müdigkeitsgesellschaft (Berlin: Matthes & Seitz).

Hannula, Mika (2004) Riwer low, mountain high. Contextualizing artistic research. In: Balkema/Slager (eds.) Artistic Research, p. 70–79.
Harrasser, Karin (2013) Körper 2.0. Über die technische Erweiterbarkeit des Menschen (Bielefeld: transcript).
Hartley, Linda (1995) Wisdom of the body moving: an introduction to body-mind centering (Berkeley: North Atlantic Books).
Hasselmann, Kristiane; Schmidt, Sandra; Zumbusch, Cornelia (eds.) (2004) Utopische Körper (München: Wilhelm Fink Verlag).
Hegel, G.W.F. (2003) The Phenomenology of Mind (Mineola, New York: Dover Publications).
Hewitt, Andrew (2005) Social Choreography. Ideology as Performance in Dance and Everyday Movement (Durham: Duke University Press).
https://www.corpusweb.net/was-ist-choreographie.html, date accessed 20 April 2022.
https://www.forbes.com/sites/thomasbrewster/2020/01/29/findface-rolls-out-huge-facial-recognition-surveillance-in-moscow-russia/, date accessed 20 April 2022.
https://www.francis-bacon.com/artworks/paintings/three-studies-human-head , date accessed 20 April 2022.
https://www.fundus-theater.de/wp-content/uploads/2017/09/brsch_showandtell.pdf, date accessed 20 April 2022.
https://www.gagapeople.com/, date accessed 20 April 2022.
https://international-acting-coach.com, date accessed 20 April 2022.
https://julireinartz.org, date accessed 20 April 2022.
https://livesandlegaciesblog.org/2016/09/15/le-pouf-sensational-hairstyle-of-the-18th-century/, date accessed 20 April 2022.
http://www.kleintechnique.com, date accessed 20 April 2022.
https://www.moma.org/learn/moma_learning/glossary/, date accessed 20 April 2022.
https://pab-research.de, date accessed 20 April 2022.
https://pab-research.de/research-map/, date accessed 20 April 2022.
http://performingcitizenship.de/data/en/, date accessed 20 April 2022.
http://performingcitizenship.de/data/en/category/forschungsprojekte/, date accessed 20 April 2022.
https://remixculture.ca/appropriation-in-pop-art/, date accessed 20 April 2022.
http://sophieaigner.de/hello/, date accessed 20 April 2022.

https://soundcloud.com/hau-hebbel-am-ufer/tumay-kilincel-artisttalk, date accessed 20 April 2022.
http://www.thebodyasarchive.com/, date accessed 20 April 2022.
https://www.thegutscompany.net/de/people/1, date accessed 20 April 2022.
https://www.theguardian.com/technology/2016/may/17/findface-face-recognition-app-end-public-anonymity-vkontakte, date accessed 20 April 2022.
http://www.urmesurveillance.com/, date accessed 20 April 2022.
https://vaniarovisco.wordpress.com/, date accessed 20 April 2022.
Kleinschmidt, Katharina (2018) Artistic Reseach als Wissensgefüge. Eine Praxeologie des Probens im Zeitgenössischen Tanz (München: epodium).
Law, Alma H.; Gordon, Mel (2012) Meyerhold, Eisenstein and Biomechanics. Actor training in Revolutionary Russia (Jefferson: McFarland).
Lenk, Elisabeth (1986) Kritische Phantasie (München: Matthes & Seitz).
Lecoq, Jaques (2003) Der poetische Körper (Berlin: Alexander Verlag).
Lepecki, André (2006) Exhausting Dance. Performance and the Politics of Movement (London, Newyork: Routledge).
Maharaj, Sarat (2004) Unfinishable sketch of "an unknown object in 4D": scenes of artistic research. In: Balkema/Slager (eds.) Artistic Research, p. 39–58.
Martin, Luther H. (ed.) (1988) Technologien des Selbst, p. 24–62 (Frankfurt: Fischer).
Marzano, Michela (2013) Philosophie des Körpers (Munich: Diederichs Verlag).
Mauss, Marcel (2010) Soziologie und Anthropologie. Band 2, p. 202. (Wiesbaden: VS Verlag für Sozialwissenschaften).
Merleau-Ponty, Maurice (2012) Phenomenology of Perception Trans. Donald Landes (London: Routledge).
Michelberger, Melodie (2021) Body politics (Hamburg: Rowohlt).
Morris, Eric (1998) Acting, Imaging and the Unconscious (Los Angeles: Ermor).
Morris, Eric; Joan Hotchkis (2002) No Acting Please (Los Angeles: Ermor).
Nelson, Maggie (2015) Die Argonauten (Berlin: Hanser Verlag).
Neuenfeld, Jörg (2005) Alles ist Spiel (Würzburg: Königshausen und Neumann).
Nida-Rümelin; Kufeld, Klaus (eds.) (2011) Die Gegenwart der Utopie. Zeitkritik und Denkwende (Freiburg, München: Verlag Karl Alber).
Noë, Alva (2006) Action in perception (Cambridge: The MIT Press).
Parry, Eugenia; Siegel, Elizabeth (eds.) (2011) Ralph Eugene Meatyard. Dolls and Masks. (Santa Fe: Radius Books).
Peters, Sybille (2011) Der Vortrag als Performance (Bielefeld: transcript).

Peters Sybille (ed.) (2013) Das Forschen aller. Artistic Research als Wissensproduktion zwischen Kunst, Wissenschaft und Gesellschaft. (Bielefeld: transcript).

Petronella Foultier, Anna; Roos, Cecilia (2013) Material of Movement and Thought. Reflections on the Dancer's Practice and Corporeality (Stockholm: Firework Edition).

Peréz Royo, Victoria; Sánchez, José A.; Blanco, Christina: In-definitions. Forschung in den performativen Künsten. In: Peters, Sibylle (2013) Das Forschen Aller. Artistic Research als Wissensproduktion zwischen Kunst, Wissenschaft und Gesellschaft, p. 23–46.

Perniola, Mario (1999) Der Sex-Appeal des Anorganischen Trans. Nicole Finsinger (Wien: Turia und Kant).

Plessner, Helmuth (2003) Conditio Humana (Berlin: Suhrkamp).

Preciado, Paul Beatriz (2013) Testo Junkie. Sex, Drugs, and Biopolitics in the Pharmacopornographic era Trans.Bruce Benderson (New York: The Feminist Press).

Raikwar, Nikita (2016) Body Positivity. Tackling Negative Body Image (independently published).

Reckwitz, Andreas (2017) The invention of creativity (Cambridge: Polity Press).

Rees, Anuschka (2019) Beyond Beautiful (Köln: DuMont).

Richardson, Irene (2012) Learn how to do automatic writing. A step by step course to help you access higher realm of the mind, body and spirit (Frederick: Crystal Forests).

Schiller, Friedrich (2014) On the Aestehtic Education of Man (New York: Angelico Press).

Schmidt Bergmann, Hansgeorg (2000) In: Rilke, Rainer Maria: Die Aufzeichnungen des Malte Laurids Brigge (Berlin: Suhrkamp).

Schneider, Christa (2012) Cindy Sherman. History Portraits (München: Schirmer, Mosel).

Seel, Martin (2001) Drei Regeln für Utopisten. In: Merkur. Deutsche Zeitschrift für europäisches Denken. Heft 9/10. 55. Jahrgang (Stuttgart: Klett-Cotta).

Sennett, Richard (1992) The fall of public man (New York, London: W.W. Norton & Company).

Sennett, Richard (1998) The corrosion of character (New York, London: W.W. Norton & Company).

Siegmund, Gerald (2004) William Forsythe. Denken in Bewegung (Berlin: Henschel).

Slager, Henk (2009) Art and Method. In: Elkins, James (ed.) Artists with PhDs. On the New Doctoral Degree in Studio Art (Washington: New Academia Publishing).
Sowa, Hubert (2012) Imagination im Bildungsprozess, p. 22–74. In: Sowa Hubert (ed). Bildung der Imagination. Band 1 (Oberhausen: Athena Verlag).
Stamer, Peter (2015) Was ist ein künstlerisches Labor? In: Gehm, Sabine; Husemann, Pirkko; von Wilcke, Katharina (eds.) Wissen in Bewegung. (Bielefeld: transcript).
Stelling, Anke (2017) Fürsorge (Berlin: Verbrecher).
Turchi, Peter (2004) Maps of the Imagination. The writer as cartographer (San Antonio: Trinity University Press).
Villa, Paula Irene (2008a) Wider die Rede vom Äußerlichen. In: Villa, Paula-Irene (ed). Schön normal. Manipulationen am Körper als Technologien des Selbst (Bielefeld: transcript).
Villa, Paula-Irene (2008b) Habe den Mut, Dich deines Körpers zu bedienen. In: Villa, Paula-Irene (ed.) Schön normal. Manipulationen am Körper als Technologien des Selbst. (Bielefeld: transcript).
Villa, Paula- Irene (2013) Prekäre Körper in prekären Zeiten – Ambivalenzen gegenwärtiger somatischer Technologien des Selbst. In: Mayer, Ralf; Thompson, Christiane; Wimmer, Michael (eds): Inszenierung und Optimierung des Selbst. Zur Analyse gegenwärtiger Selbsttechnologien (Wiesbaden: Springer).
Waldenfels, Bernhard (2006) Grundmotive einer Phänomenologie des Fremden (Berlin: Suhrkamp).
Waldenfels, Bernhard (1997) Topographie des Fremden (Berlin: Suhrkamp).
Wellman, H. M.; Harris, P. L.; Banerjee, M.; Sinclair, A. (1995). Early understanding of emotion: evidence from natural language. Cognition and Emotion, 9(2/3), p. 117–149.
Wells, Samuel Roberts (1888) How to Read Character: a New Illustrated Handbook of Phrenology and Physiognomy, for Students and Examiners (New York: Fowler & Wells).
Zapora, Ruth (1995) Action Theater: The Improvisation of Presence (Berkeley: North Atlantic Books).
Zapora, Ruth (2014) Improvisation On the Edge: Notes from On and Off the Stage (Berkeley: North Atlantic Books).

Image Credits

p. 65: Loloi, Yossi (2010) The full beauty project. Cf. http://www.yossiloloi.com/portfolio/fullbeauty-project/ (date accessed 9 February 2022).

p. 74–76, p. 87: Velsinger, Antje (2016) Research documentation.

p. 82: Stach, Jiri (1980) Krajina c.76. Cf. https://www.jiristach.cz/en/photos-8oies.php (date accessed 9 February 2022).

p. 90–92, p. 107–109, p. 117, p. 121–124: Weiss, Margaux (2016) Documentation of Research presentation "The bodies we are".

p. 102: Kahn, Brian (creative director) & LHGFX (photography) BODIES OF WORK. Vol.1. Cf. https://www.bodybuilding.com/fun/bodies-of-work.html (date accessed 9 February 2022).

p. 127: Coiffure à l'indépendance ou Le triomphe de la liberté. Anonymous circa 1778. Found on: https://museefrancoamericain.fr/collection/objet/coiffure-de-lindependanceou-le-triomphe-de-la-liberte (date accessed 9 February 2022).

p. 141–142, p. 155–158, p. 162: Sophie Aigner (2017) Research documentation.

p. 163, p. 167–170, p. 176–178, p. 183: Weiss, Margaux (2017) Documentation of Research presentation "Let's face it!".

Printed in the USA
CPSIA information can be obtained
at www.ICGtesting.com
JSHW012013100624
64547JS00029B/205